SOCIOLINGUISTICS

a brief introduction...

Joshua A. Fishman

NEWBURY HOUSE LANGUAGE SERIES

SOCIOLINGUISTICS

A BRIEF INTRODUCTION

Joshua A. Fishman
Yeshiva University

NEWBURY HOUSE PUBLISHERS,   ROWLEY, MASSACHUSETTS

SOCIOLINGUISTICS

A BRIEF INTRODUCTION

Joshua A. Fishman
Yeshiva University

NEWBURY HOUSE PUBLISHERS, ROWLEY, MASSACHUSETTS

NEWBURY HOUSE PUBLISHERS, INC.

LANGUAGE SCIENCE
LANGUAGE LEARNING
LANGUAGE TEACHING

68 Middle Road, Rowley, Massachusetts 01969

First Printing:	June, 1970
Second Printing:	August, 1971
Third Printing:	February, 1972
Fourth Printing:	January, 1975

Library of Congress Card Number: 73-109101

ISBN: 912066-01-6.

Printed in the United States of America.

FOREWORD

The idea of systematic study of language as a social phenomenon is not new. Long ago prominent social psychologists like George Herbert Mead emphasized the importance of language in social interaction, and in the early years of the century prominent linguists like Antoine Meillet tried to place language in its social setting and to combine social analysis with the investigation of language change. Linguistics has also traditionally had a place within anthropological research. But in spite of the recognition of language as a social phenomenon and the connection between linguistics and anthropology, the methods and insights of the social sciences and those of linguistics have generally gone their separate ways. It is only within the last ten to fifteen years that a number of scholars have combined concepts and research techniques from sociology, social psychology, and linguistics in the study of certain kinds of language behavior. This new field of sociolinguistics, as it is called, is far from unified in goals, techniques, or levels of analysis. Also, as might be expected, its practitioners are often linguistic scholars or social scientists whose primary research work is in other fields but who are drawn to sociolinguistic problems because of their relation to issues of theory in their respective fields.

The brief introduction to sociolinguistics which Joshua Fishman has written manages to cover a great many different trends of research, different levels of analysis, and quite different theoretical concerns. Students generally report that every introductory course in Sociolinguistics is unique, being based on the particular research interests of the sociolinguist, anthropologist, or linguist who happens to teach it. In this introduction, however, Fishman has tried not only to represent all the major streams of research but also to integrate them as far as this can be done in the present state of sociolinguistic theory. In doing so he has succeeded in giving an unusually well balanced conspectus of the whole field. One reason for his success is probably the fact that he is one of the very small number of scholars for whom sociolinguistic research and teaching are primary rather than marginal or incidental to other work.

Professor Fishman's interest in sociolinguistics, or the sociology of language as he sometimes prefers to call it, ranges from large questions of language use at the national or international level to detailed investigations of personal interaction, and in his publications the methods represented have ranged from the interpretation of census data to linguistic analysis of bilingual conversations. In fact, one of the most characteristic features of Fishman's work has been his willingness to use methods of the most varied kinds to achieve the results he wants. He has combined diachronic and synchronic approaches, and techniques drawn from sociology, psychology, and linguistics. In a series of studies of the language behavior of ethnic groups in the United States he has not only contributed to general questions such as the study of bilingualism and the relation of language to nationalism, but in his use of such concepts as language maintenance and shift and domains of language use he has taken important first steps toward the development of a sociolinguistic theory of societal multilingualism. In addition to his numerous articles and monographs, Professor Fishman is the senior editor and major author of three substantial books in sociolinguistics, Language Loyalty in the United States, Language Problems of Developing Nations, *and* Bilingualism in the Barrio, *and he is undoubtedly one of the best qualified people to prepare an introduction to the field.*

Like any new interdisciplinary field, sociolinguistics is full of the excitement of unexpected discoveries and the stimulation of finding connections between previously unrelated theories or disciplines. It comes as a surprise to both the linguist and the sociologist when William Labov shows that linguistic variables are among the most precise and predictable indicators of socioeconomic status in New York City. The social psychologist is surprised by the great variety of pronoun systems of address in the world's languages, but the linguist is even more surprised when Roger Brown shows that much of this variation can be interpreted within a very limited number of social dimensions. The psychologist who is convinced of the disadvantages of bilingualism for the individual is taken aback by the demonstrated prevalence of bilingualism among the elites of many societies. And so it goes, with surprises for political scientists, dialectologists, and social scientists of all kinds who have paid little attention to the functions of differing speech varieties in human communities. Fishman does not emphasize the exciting and upsetting nature of much sociolinguistic research, but it shows through his calm reporting sufficiently to communicate the attraction sociolinguistics has for many of its proponents.

As often happens with a new field, the output of publications in sociolinguistics is largely in specialized studies rather than comprehensive handbooks or solid textbooks. The handful of existing introductory textbooks on sociolinguistics or the sociology of language tend to be poorly balanced in coverage, superficial in treatment, and premature in their generalizations and conclusions. The student who wants some kind of overview must be content with anthologies and collections of readings, and here the volumes of Hymes, Bright, Hymes and Gumperz, and Fishman offer a rich selection of articles and extracts for him to study. Several of the leading sociolinguists are known to be writing introductory textbooks, and we can hope that in several years' time we will have adequate coverage of the field. For the present, however, we have only such longish review essays as those of Ervin-Tripp, Grimshaw, and Gumperz. For some time to come the Fishman introduction, also originally written as a kind of review essay, will provide the most useful summary of the field for those who want to find out about it.

Fishman has chosen to begin his presentation with a strong dose of linguistics. We could imagine several motivations for this choice. He may have wanted to frighten off the social scientist who is interested but is unwilling to look at language behavior in the careful, technical way sociolinguistic research requires. Or he may have wanted to show that in this field a non-linguist like himself deals with linguistic analysis just as a linguist must deal with various kinds of social analysis. Whatever his motivation, I think he made the right choice. The student of social science who becomes interested in language behavior has generally had little or no background in linguistics and there is no other place he can turn for a quick introduction designed to show people like him how linguistics might be of use in following up his interest. On the other hand, the linguist who becomes interested in the social functions of language often has some social science background in his education and is likely to be highly skeptical about a sociolinguistic treatise which does not immediately demonstrate some linguistic sophistication. The social scientist will acquire a smattering of linguistics and perhaps a little respect for it, and the linguist will be lured on to the sociolinguistic theory and research methods which are more fundamental to his own discipline than he realizes.

Finally, Fishman's introduction differs from most of the existing review articles and books in the field by having a section on applied sociolinguistics. Most researchers in sociolinguistics would take the position of many social scientists that their findings are too fragmentary and have too inadequate a theoretical framework to be available for application to social problems. It is refreshing to have a research scholar admit the inconclusiveness of the findings in his field but consider them relevant to problems in society and favor using them to the extent possible in attempting solutions to the problems. But perhaps this is not surprising when the scholar is the editor of the Journal of Social Issues.

It is my hope that this little book and its carefully selected bibliography will introduce many students to the rapidly developing field of sociolinguistics and in time will add substantially to the number of people for whom sociolinguistic research and application offers an interesting and rewarding career.

Addis Ababa   *Charles A. Ferguson*
December 1969

PREFACE

The purpose of this brief introduction to sociolinguistics is to familiarize the student of linguistics with the social context of speech, and to familiarize the student of society with language as a referent and dimension of social behavior. It attempts to conceptually integrate the sociolinguistics literature—emphasizing that which appeared in the mid and late 1960's—so that micro-sociolinguistics, and macro-sociolinguistics, and applied sociolinguistics can be understood in relation to each other, rather than as disparate levels or topics of analysis.

The material here presented to the reader has been tried out on students at several universities. It stresses the need to take seriously both linguistic and societal analysis, giving priority to neither, adopting methods from all of the behavioral sciences, interrelating theories and methods that have too often been isolated from each other, and setting aside as unfounded those that claim to be self-sufficient for all problems whatsoever.

Sociolinguistics is a relatively new interdisciplinary field. It will change rapidly in the years immediately ahead. This introduction, it is hoped, will contribute to the ultimate shape of the field by stimulating rather than restricting its continued growth.

New York City   *Joshua A. Fishman*
January, 1970

ACKNOWLEDGEMENTS

For their many helpful comments and corrections I am greatly indebted to Robert Cooper (Yeshiva), Charles Ferguson (Stanford), Richard Howell (Richmond College, City University of New York), Björn Jernudd (Monash), and Joan Rubin (George Washington), each of whom was kind enough to read a preliminary draft of this material.

CONTENTS

INTRODUCTION   1

SECTION I
LINGUISTICS: THE SCIENCE OF CODE DESCRIPTION
... AND MORE   5

    1.1 Descriptive Linguistics   6
    1.2 Other Branches of Linguistics   13

SECTION II
SOME BASIC SOCIOLINGUISTIC CONCEPTS   21

    2.1 Language–Dialect–Variety   21
    2.2 Major Types of Attitude and Behavior
        Toward Language   24
    2.3 Speech Community   28

SECTION III
INTERACTIONAL SOCIOLINGUISTICS: MICRO
AND MACRO   37

    3.1 How Should Talk Be Contextually Described   41
    3.2 Microlevel Analysis in Sociolinguistics   43
    3.3 Role Relationships   44
    3.4 The Situation: Congruent and Incongruent   47
    3.5 The Transition to Marco-sociolinguistics   51
    3.6 Sociolinguistics: Multilevel and Multimethod   54

SECTION IV
SOCIETAL DIFFERENTIATION AND REPERTOIRE
RANGE   57

    4.1 The Significance of Pervasive Linguistic
        Discontinuity   61
    4.2 More Marginal Systematic Discontinuity   63
    4.3 Nonproletarians of All Regions, Unite!   67
    4.4 Diversification vs. Massification   69

SECTION V
SOCIETAL BILINGUALISM: STABLE AND
TRANSITIONAL   73

    5.1 Diglossia   73
    5.2 Speech Communities Characterized by
        Both Diglossia and Bilingualism   75
    5.3 Diglossia Without Bilingualism   81
    5.4 Bilingualism Without Diglossia   83
    5.5 Neither Diglossia Nor Bilingualism   88
    5.6 Conclusions   89

SECTION VI
SOCIOCULTURAL ORGANIZATION: LANGUAGE
CONSTRAINTS AND LANGUAGE REFLECTIONS   91

    6.1 Grammatical Structure Constrains
        Cognition   92
    6.2 Lexical Structure Constrains Cognition   96
    6.3 Lexical Structure Reflects Social
        Organization   102

SECTION VII
APPLIED SOCIOLINGUISTICS   107

    7.1 The Formulation of Language Policy   108
    7.2 The Implementation of Language Policy   109
    7.3 Language Planning   109
    7.4 Educational Applications   110
    7.5 The Rationalization of Language Decisions   111

DR. FERGUSON'S REFERENCES   113

BIBLIOGRAPHY   115

INTRODUCTION

Newspaper headlines with all their stridency may serve to remind us of a truism that is too frequently overlooked by too many Americans, namely, that language is not merely a *means* of interpersonal communication and influence. It is not merely a *carrier* of content, whether latent or manifest. Language itself *is* content, a referent for loyalties and animosities, an indicator of social statuses and personal relationships, a marker of situations and topics as well as of the societal goals and the large-scale value-laden arenas of interaction that typify every speech community.

Any speech community of even moderate complexity reveals several varieties of language, all of which are functionally differentiated from each other. In some cases the varieties may represent different occupational or interest specializations ("shop talk," "hippie talk," etc.) and, therefore, contain vocabulary, pronunciations, and phraseology which are not generally used or even known throughout the broader speech community. As a result, the speakers of specialized varieties may not always employ them. Not only must they switch to other varieties of language when they interact in less specialized (or differently specialized) networks within the broader speech community of which they are a part, but most of them do not even use their specialized varieties all of the time with one another. On some occasions, interlocutors who *can* speak a particular specialized variety to one another nevertheless do not do so, but instead switch to a different variety of language which is either in wider use or which is indicative of quite a different set of interests and relationships than is associated with their specialized variety. This type of switching represents the raw data of sociolinguistics, the discipline that seeks to determine (among other things) who speaks what variety of what language to whom, when, and concerning what.

The varieties of language that exist within a speech community need not all represent occupational or interest specializations. Some varieties may represent social-class (economic, educational, ethnic) distinctions within coterritorial populations. "Brooklynese" and "Cockney" English within New York and London, respectively, do not connote foreignness or even a particular section of the city so much as lower-class status in terms of income, education, or ethnicity. Nevertheless, many individuals who have left lower-class status behind can and do switch back and forth between Brooklynese and more regionally standard New York English when speaking to each other, depending on their feelings toward each other, the topic under discussion, where they happen to be when they are conversing, and several other factors, all of which can exhibit variation and, as a result, can be signaled by switching from one variety of English to another.

A speech community that has available to it several varieties of language may be said to possess a *verbal repertoire.* Such repertoires may not only consist of different specialized varieties and different social-class varieties, but may also reveal different regional varieties (Boston English, Southern English, Midwestern English, and other widely, and roughly, designated dialects of American English are regional varieties), if the speech community is sufficiently large so that enclaves come to arise within it on a geographic basis alone.

Furthermore, multilingual speech communities may employ, for the purposes of *intragroup* communication, all of the above types or varieties of language within each of the codes that the community recognizes as "distinct" languages (e.g., within Yiddish *and* Hebrew, among most pre-World War II Eastern European Jews; within English and Hindi, among many upper-class individuals in India today, etc.).

Regardless of the nature of the language varieties involved in the verbal repertoire of a speech community (occupational, social class, regional, etc.) and regardless of the interaction between them (for initially regional dialects may come to represent social varieties as well, and vice versa) sociolinguistics seeks to describe their linguistic and functional characteristics. However, sociolinguistics also seeks to do much more. It seeks to determine how much of the entire speech community's verbal repertoire is available to various smaller interaction networks within that community, since the entire verbal repertoire of a speech community may be more extensive than the verbal repertoire controlled by subgroups within that community. Sociolinguistics seeks to trace the linguistic influences of the varieties on each other. It seeks to determine how changes in the fortunes and interactions of networks of speakers alter the ranges (complexity) of their verbal repertoires. All in all, sociolinguistics seeks to discover the societal rules or norms that explain and constrain language behavior and the behavior toward language in speech communities.

Sociolinguistics also seeks to determine the symbolic value of language varieties for their speakers. That language varieties come to have symbolic or symptomatic value, in and of themselves, is an inevitable consequence of their functional differentiation. If certain varieties are indicative of certain interests, of certain backgrounds, or of certain origins, they come to represent the ties and aspirations, the limitations and the opportunities with which these interests, backgrounds, and origins, in turn, are associated. Language varieties rise and fall in symbolic value as the status of their most characteristic or marked functions rises and falls. Varieties come to represent intimacy and equality if they are most typically learned and employed in interactions that stress such bonds between interlocutors. Other varieties come to represent educated status or national identification as a result of the attainments associated with their use and their users and as a result of their utilization in situations and relationships that pertain to formal learning or to particular ideologies. However, these functions are capable of change (and of being consciously changed), just as the linguistic features of the varieties themselves may change (and may be consciously changed), and just as the demographic distribution of users of a variety within a particular speech community may change.

Sociolinguistics is the study of the characteristics of language varieties, the characteristics of their functions, and the characteristics of their speakers as these three constantly interact, change, and change one another within a speech community.

Section I

LINGUISTICS:
THE SCIENCE OF CODE
DESCRIPTION . . . AND MORE

If one part of sociolinguistics comprises the "study of the characteristics of language varieties" then we must turn to that science that has specialized in the systematic description of language: linguistics. To attempt to describe and analyze language data, in this day and age, without a knowledge of linguistic concepts and methods is to be as primitive as to try to describe and analyze human behavior more generally (or the functions of language varieties and the characteristics of their speakers) without knowledge of psychological and sociological concepts and methods.

It is no more possible to provide an adequate introduction to linguistics "in one easy lesson" than to provide one for sociology or psychology. Nevertheless, it may be possible to briefly sketch some of the major concerns and methods of linguistics that bear upon sociolinguistics. The purpose of the next few pages, therefore, is to bring about "linguistics appreciation," and of a very selective sort at that, rather than to present a full-fledged introduction to a very technical and complicated science which intersects the humanities, the social sciences, and the natural sciences in its various subdivisions. The specialist knows full well that "music appreciation" is not the same as music mastery. Similarly, "linguistics appreciation" is not the same as linguistics mastery. Nevertheless, it is a beginning.

As a formal discipline, particularly in so far as the American academic scene is concerned, linguistics is a very recent field of specialization. The Linguistic Society of America was founded only in 1924. (The oldest linguistic society in the world, that of Paris, was founded in 1864.) Even today, when the number of linguists and linguistics programs in American universities is greater than ever before, there are only some twoscore graduate linguistics departments in the United States. Nevertheless, this discipline has not only come to be of prime interest to a growing band of dedicated scholars and practitioners within linguistics per se, but it has also in very recent years forcefully come to the attention of all other disciplines that recognize the centrality of verbal interaction in human affairs. Interdisciplinary contacts between linguistics and anthropology have been well established since the very appearance of linguistics in American universities. The anthropological linguist is a well-recognized and highly regarded specialist among linguists and anthropologists alike. Indeed, linguistics is recognized as a "branch" of anthropology in many textbooks and training programs. Of more recent vintage is psycholinguistics. Most recent of all is sociolinguistics, an interdisciplinary field which is just now beginning to train specialists that can bridge linguistics and sociology-social psychology in such a manner as to expand the horizons of both.

1.1 DESCRIPTIVE LINGUISTICS

The basic field in which most (if not all) linguists have been trained is that which is known as descriptive or synchronic linguistics. As its names imply, this field focuses upon the systematic description of a given language in a given time and place. It is not historical; it is not comparative; it is not prescriptive. Its emphasis is definitely on *spoken language,* the assumption being that written language is both derivative and different from natural language or speech.

It is common for the uninitiated to think of a language as being well represented by an unabridged dictionary. This view implies that the way to describe a language is to consider its components to be words. Any careful or consistent and exhaustive presentation and definition of the words of a language (which may be exactly what dictionaries attempt to do) would, therefore, from this point of view, be considered a description of that language. For most linguists, however, there are two other kinds of systematic presentations which are considered even more basic to their goal of describing language: the sound system of a language and the grammatical system of that language.

The branch of linguistics that is concerned with the systematic description of the sounds (phones) of a language is *phonology.* Some of the more general subspecialties within phonology are articulatory phonetics (how tongue, lips, teeth, vocal chords, velum, nasal passage, and other speech organs produce the sounds of language) and acoustic phonetics (the physical properties of the sound waves or signals emitted by the speaker). Linguists have devised for purposes of phonetic notation the International Phonetic Alphabet, which is roughly adequate for the transcription of speech in all languages, although minor adjustments or additions to it are required in most individual cases.

On the foundation of these more general branches of phonology linguistics has been able to establish the study of *phonemics,* i.e., the study of those sounds that enter into meaningful contrasts or combinations in a given language, as compared to all of the physically differentiable sounds of a language (which are of interest in *phonetics*). A skilled phonetician differentiates far more fine shades of language sounds than do the native speakers of any particular language. Phonetic analysis is now sufficiently refined to demonstrate that no two speakers of a given language pronounce their words in exactly the same way. Indeed, the degree of refinement available to phonetic analysis has gone so far that it is possible to show that even an idiolect (the way of speaking that characterizes an individual) is not entirely consistent. The same individual does not pronounce the same word in the same way on all occasions of the same type. Into this endless series of successively refined analysis of language sound differences *phonemics* seeks to introduce the parsimony that derives from a knowledge of those sound differences that are meaningfully distinctive (i.e., that serve to distinguish between linguistic signs and their meanings) for the native speakers of a particular language. The following brief example may illustrate the phonemic approach to demonstrable phonetic differences.

Let us consider the "b" sound in English, Arabic, and Bengali. That each of these languages has some sound that the American man in the street would unhesitatingly represent by the letter *b* is, for linguistics, a nonstructural comment, and therefore one of no particular interest. It *is* of interest, however, to point out that in English *aba* and *apa* are differentiated, the voiced bilabial stop ("b") in the first being considered clearly different from the unvoiced bilabial stop ("p") in the second because the difference between *b* and *p* is crucial to recognizing the difference in meaning between "bit" and "pit," "bet" and "pet," and hundreds of other meaningful contrasts. In Arabic, on the other hand, no such meaningful substitutions of *b* and *p* are made. The native speaker of Arabic says only *aba* and uses a *p* sound only under special conditions, such as before *s* or *t*. Whatever sound differences exist in the *p-b* range in Arabic are not distinctive, i.e., they do not signal meaning differences, and are therefore referred to as allophones.

Thus, it is not enough to say that both English and Arabic have a *b* sound, for the sound functions far differently in the two languages. In English *b* and *p* function as phonemically different sounds (and, therefore, are notated /p/ and /b/); in Arabic they do not.

The absence or presence of a meaningful contrast between *b* and *p* takes on even greater linguistic significance if Bengali is examined. Not only are /b/ and /p/ differentiated by the ordinary native speaker of Bengali, but in addition, an *unaspirated p* (as in the English *spin*) is differentiated from an *aspirated p* (as in the English *pin*). Similarly, an *unaspirated b* is regularly differentiated from an *aspirated b*.

Note that while English recognizes a phonemic (meaning-related) difference between two sounds (one voiced and one unvoiced) that represent only a meaningless difference in Arabic, Bengali recognizes a further phonemic difference between two pairs of sounds (each with an aspirated and an unaspirated component) that represent only meaningless phonetic differences in English. Furthermore, as the English and Bengali languages change over time, changes in their "b" sounds will presumably be correlated with changes in their "p" sounds, precisely because these sounds are systematically related to each other.

It is in this last respect—i.e., in terms of systematic interrelationships—that descriptive linguistics is interested in the sounds of a language. This is also why descriptive linguistics is sometimes referred to as structural linguistics. It is not merely the sounds of a language that are of interest to linguistics, nor even the meaningfully different sounds, but above all, the systematic links that exist between the meaningfully different sounds of a language. The phonemes of a language, like all other features of a language at a given point in time, are part of a system (a "structure") that operates as a whole. Changes in one part of the structure affect the other parts; indeed, in true Gestalt fashion, any phonemic part can be truly appreciated only in terms of the phonological whole. Saussure (1916) emphasized that language is a system in which every part has its interlinked place ("un systeme où tout se tient") and this structural dictum has since come to characterize not only descriptive linguistics but other branches as well.

So basic is descriptive linguistics to linguistic science as a whole that another example of its concerns, this time at the level of grammatical analysis, is in order. Such an example is particularly desirable because the grammatical structure of language is completely interwoven with its sound structure, so much so that some linguists claim that phonological analysis depends on and must be part of an exhaustive grammatical analysis (although most linguists consider phonology, grammar, lexicon, and semantics as quite separate *levels* of analysis).

Just as there is a minimal unit of meaningful sound (actually, of substitutionally meaningful sound, since the sounds in question are not meaningful per se), the phoneme, so is there a minimal unit of meaningful grammatical (i.e., of ordered or environmental) form, the *morpheme.* As a result, one branch of grammatical study is known as *morphology.* It studies the ordered relationships between small meaningful segments such as occur within words. (Syntax, on the other hand, studies the ordered relationships between units such as words in a phrase or utterance.) Thus, many English verbs form the past tense by adding a morpheme, which may be represented as [d], to the present tense of the verb: I open—I opened. [d] means past tense in English. Similarly, many English nouns form their plural by adding a morpheme, which may be represented as [z], to their singular: car—cars. In both of these instances, however, the morphemes in question occur in several different forms that also differ somewhat as to their sound. Functionally equivalent alternatives of the same morpheme are referred to as *allomorphs,* precisely because there is no functional difference between them, however much they may differ in sound, just as sounds that revealed no functional difference were referred to earlier as *allophones.* The allomorphs of [d] for the common, productive English verbs may sound like a *d* (as in opened), like a *t* (as in laughed), or like *ed* (as in mended). However, these allomorphs are not used at random. How would linguistics provide a rule to indicate when the native speaker of English employs which? What would such a rule be like?

To begin with, linguists would list as many verbs as possible that utilize each variant of the [d] morpheme. Such a list might initially look like that shown in Table 1. After inspecting the array of final sounds in each of the columns of that table a linguist is able to do that which no ordinary native speaker of English can do: formulate a very few rules which summarize the systematic variation in the three allomorphs of [d]. Such rules might proceed as follows:

TABLE 1. Allomorphs of $\{d\}$ in the Past Tense of Some Common, Productive English Verbs.

ed	*t*	*d*
mend	bank	open
lift	cook	use
boot	drop	save
raid	help	bomb
kid	walk	mail
tend	laugh	try
sift	shop	play
hoot	stamp	radio
shade	rank	hinge
hand	staff	rig

1. If the verb stem ends in /t/ or /d/ the past tense ends in *ed,* (with the exception of a small number of verbs that retain the same form in past and present: cut, hit, put),

2. If the verb stem ends in a voiceless stop (other than /t/) or in a voiceless spirant, the past tense ends in *t,*

3. Otherwise, the past tense ends in *d.*

The above three brief rules pertain to the phonological conditioning of allomorphs. The allomorphs of [d] are realized according to their phonological environment. Thus, variations in grammatical form and variations in phonological form may and frequently do coincide. In general, linguistics has traditionally pursued two kinds of structured variation: variation relatable to change in meaning (such as the substitutional meaning that underlies phonemic analysis) and variation relatable to change in environment (such as the positional meaning that underlies morphemic analysis). Further synchronic variation in language, i.e., variation that cannot be identified either with change in meaning (i.e., change in referent) or with change in linguistic environment, when geographic area is held constant, has traditionally been thought of as "free variation," i.e., as variation (not to say "irregularity") due to factors outside of *langue* (the latent structure underlying speech) and therefore outside of the descriptive rules pertaining to *langue.* It is in some of the kinds of free variation—in variations which may co-occur with differences in a speaker's alertness or emotional state, with differences in topic, role relationship, communicational setting, or interpersonal purpose—that sociolinguistics (and other interdisciplinary studies of language usage) attempts to discover additional regularity.

Linguistics has long been aware that "free variation" might have a structure of its own. However, *that* structure (when and if it obtains) has usually been considered as being part of the structure of the speech event rather than part of the structure of the speech code per se. Although descriptive linguistics has emphasized the spoken language, the *speech act* itself was long considered to be outside of the domain of linguistics, for the speech act, just like the message content of speech, was considered to be part of "communication" (long considered by linguists to be an outer or surface phenomenon) rather than part and parcel of *langue* per se (the heart of the matter). Many famous linguists have warned against confusing the two.

Thus, if it appeared that certain phonemic, morphological, syntactic, or lexical regularities were not *always* as regular as one would hope (time and place remaining constant), this was attributed to the irregularity of *parole* (speaking, behavioral realization) as distinct from the systematic and abstract purity of *langue* (language, underlying structure) with which linguists should really be concerned. *Parole* is subject to many factors that produce variation (among those not previously mentioned: fatigue, anger, limitation in memory span, interruptions, etc.). These are all factors of "degree," of "more or less," of "sometimes." It was thought that the goal of linguistics was to cut through these psychological and sociological sources of "static" and to concern itself with matters that were clear-cut enough to be viewed as all or none phenomena: the basic code which, at any given time and place, might be considered to be one and the same for all who employed it. Thus, not only were linguists warned to distinguish sharply between *parole* and *langue* (de Saussure 1916), but they were also admonished to keep their distance from psychological or sociological data and theories which were viewed as inherently more concerned with the highly variable and seemingly irregular processes of verbal interaction and communication (and, therefore, with the messy data of *parole*) than with the pure code underlying these processes (Bloomfield 1933). It is only in more recent days, when the traditionally rigid distinction between *langue* and *parole* has come to be re-examined and when the varying interaction between them has come to be pursued that larger groups of linguists and of social scientists have found things to say to each other.

1.2 OTHER BRANCHES OF LINGUISTICS

Other branches of linguistics—some of them older than descriptive linguistics (even though the latter has come to be so central to all linguistic pursuits)—have long been on friendlier terms with the social sciences. *Historical* (diachronic) *linguistics,* for example, in studying the changes that occur in a given code over time (sound changes, grammatical changes, and word changes) has of necessity been interested in human migrations, intergroup contacts (conquest, trade), and any other diversification within a speech community that leads some of its members to interact with each other differentially (rather than equally or randomly), or that leads some of its members to interact with outsiders much more than do the rest. Historical linguistics (also known as *comparative linguistics*) focuses on tracing how one, earlier, parent ("proto") code subsequently divided into several related but separate ("sister" or "daughter") codes or, alternatively, how several codes were derived from one pre-existing code. Although time is the crucial dimension in the development of *families of languages* between which *genetic relationships* can be shown to exist, as it is in the reconstruction of all common ancestries, nevertheless historical linguists realize full well that the language changes that occurred were due to differential interaction and contact processes that happened as time passed, rather than to the mere passing of time per se. As a result, historical linguistics has interacted fruitfully with history, archeology, and anthropology and with other disciplines that can provide information concerning coterritorial influences between populations. In recent years, the fluctuating interaction between *langue* and *parole* (e.g., how one of the alternative systems of speaking available to a speech community spreads through the entire speech community and, increasingly displacing other alternatives, becomes an unvarying part of its basic code) has been studied by linguists working with social-science concepts and methods of data collection and data analysis on what would once have been considered a "purely" comparative problem (Labov 1963; Haugen 1961). The ties between comparative linguistics and the social sciences become stronger as the *dynamics* of language change come under increasing linguistic scrutiny, as distinct from the static, step-wise contrasts between the written records of one century and those of another that formerly dominated this field of study.

Another branch of linguistics that has frequently maintained close ties to the social sciences is *dialectology* (also known as *linguistic* or *dialect geography*). In contrast to historical linguistics this branch is concerned with variation in language on some dimension *other than time.* The achronic dimension with which dialectologists have most commonly been concerned has been geographic space or distance. Languages that are employed over considerable expanses are often spoken somewhat differently (or even quite differently) in different parts of their speech areas. These differences may be phonological, such as President Kennedy's "Cuber" (for Cuba) and "vigah" (for vigor), where a Philadelphian would have said "Cubah" and "vigor," while many a Southerner would have said "Cubah" and "vigah." Dialect differences may also apply to the lexicon (milk shake vs. frappe; soda vs. pop) and even to parts of the grammatical system. Dialectologists have traditionally prepared *linguistic atlases* to show the geographic distribution of the linguistic features that have been of interest to them. Such atlases consist of maps on which are indicated the geographical limits within which certain usages are current. These limits are known as isoglosses (Weinreich, U. 1962; Herzog 1965).

However, dialectologists are well aware that the variations that are of interest to them are not due to geographical distance per se, but rather to the interactional consequences of geographic and other kinds of "distance." Phonological, lexical, and grammatical uniformity may obtain over large geographic expanses when settlement is simultaneous and when verbal interaction as well as common identification is frequent. On the other hand, major language differences (sometimes referred to as "social dialects" or "sociolects") may arise and be maintained within relatively tiny geographic areas (e.g., in many cities) where the above conditions do not obtain. Considerations such as these have led many dialectologists, particularly those who have been interested in urban language situations, to be concerned with educational, occupational, religious, ethnic, and other social groups and societal processes (although all or most of these groups may, in part, be traceable to originally diverse geographic origins) rather than with geographic distance per se. As a result, the ties between dialectologists and social scientists (not to mention sociolinguists) have been many and strong, particularly in recent years (Blanc 1964; Ferguson and Gumperz 1960), when the entire speech act—rather than merely the code rules abstracted from the speech act—has come to be of interest to an increasing number of dialectologists (Hymes 1962).

Of late, many linguists have taken to examining the structure of language—rather than the structure of particular languages—and to doing so in order to discover the nature of those fundamental human capacities which make for the competence of native speakers. Native speakers possess a rare gift which they themselves usually overlook: the ability to generate sentences that are recognized as structurally acceptable in their speech communities, and what is more, to generate only such sentences. Many linguists now believe that a linguistic theory that can specify an adequate grammar (i.e., the rules that native speakers implicitly grasp and that constitute their native-speaker competence) will also specify the language-acquiring and language-using nature of man. These linguists say that only an adequate theory of human capacity to acquire and use language will yield an adequate theory of what language itself is (Chomsky 1957, 1965).

Sociolinguistics may ultimately serve similarly basic purposes in the on-going quest of the social sciences to understand communicative competence as a fundamental aspect of the social nature of man. The sociolinguistic theory that can specify adequate communicative competence (i.e., the rules that native members of speech communities implicitly grasp and that constitute their native member sociolinguistic behavior) will also specify the nature of social man as an acquirer and utilizer of a repertoire of verbal and behavioral skills. Man does not acquire or use his communicative competence in a single-code or single-norm community. Indeed, pervasively homogeneous communities with respect to communicative and other social behaviors do not exist except in the simplified worlds of some theorists and experimenters. Ultimately, sociolinguistics hopes to go beyond comfortably simple theory concerning the nature of communicative competence in the conviction that only an adequate theory of human capacity to acquire and to use a repertoire of interlocking language varieties and their related behaviors will yield an adequate theory of what communicative competence in social man really is.

Just as there are branches of linguistics that seek to study *langue* and *langue* alone (indeed, to study language at its "deepest," most abstract, and, therefore, at its socially most uninvolved), so are there branches of linguistics that have departed from a strict separation between *langue* and *parole* (since *parole* too has its very definite structure, since *parole* constantly influences *langue,* and since the individual's meaningful differentiation must be referred to, even though these are outside of *langue* per se, in order to establish a description of phonemic and other distinctions). Similarly, some branches of social psychology (and other social sciences as well) have moved closer to linguistics. Many sociologists and social psychologists now realize (whereas few did so a decade ago) that the norms that apply to and that may be thought of as generating human verbal interaction pertain not only to the communicative *content* and *context* of that interaction but to its linguistic *form* as well. As linguistics is developing outward—in the hopes of some: to become an all-encompassing science of language behavior—sociology and social psychology are developing toward increasing technical competence in connection with language description and analysis. Sociolinguistics is one of the by-products of these two complementary developments. Let us, therefore, now venture into sociolinguistics proper, referring to the work of linguists as necessary, but attending also to those topics that are essentially sociological and social psychological and to which few linguists have, as yet, paid much attention.

READING LIST: INTRODUCTION TO LINGUISTICS

I. *Popular Introductions and Overviews*

1. Hall, Robert A., Jr. *Linguistics and Your Language.* Doubleday, New York, 1960.
2. Ornstein, Jacob, and Wm. W. Gage. *The ABC's of Language and Linguistics.* Chilton, Philadelphia, 1964.
3. Bolinger, Dwight. *Aspects of Language.* Harcourt, Brace & World, New York, 1967.

II. *Representative American Texts*

1. Bloomfield, Leonard. *Language.* Holt, New York, 1933.
2. Gleason, H. A., Jr. *An Introduction to Descriptive Linguistics* (rev.). Holt, New York, 1961.
3. Hockett, Charles F. *A Course in Modern Linguistics* (rev.). Macmillan, New York, 1963.
4. Sapir, Edward. *Language.* Harcourt, Brace, New York, 1921. (Paperback: Harvest Books, New York, 1955).

III. *One Classic and Three Recent European Texts*

1. de Saussure, Ferdinand. *Course in General Linguistics* (translation of 1916 French original by Wade Baskin). Philosophical Library, New York, 1959.
2. Martinet, Andre. *Elements of General Linguistics* (translation of 1960 French original by Elisabeth Palmer). University of Chicago Press, Chicago, 1964.
3. Halliday, M. A. K., Angus McIntosh, and Peter Strevens. *The Linguistics Sciences and Language Teaching.* Longmans, Green, London, 1964.
4. Robins, Robert H. *General Linguistics: An Introductory Survey.* Indiana University Press, Bloomington, 1966.

IV. A Newer ("transformationalist") Approach

1. Bach, Emmon W. *An Introduction to Transformational Grammars.* Holt, New York, 1964.
2. Chomsky, Noam. *Aspects of the Theory of Syntax.* MIT Press, Cambridge, Mass., 1965.
3. Langacker, Ronald W. *Language And its Structure.* Harcourt, New York, 1968.

V. Journals to Glance at

1. *Language*
2. *Lingua*
3. *Linguistics*
4. *Linguistic Reporter*
5. *International Journal of American Linguistics*

VI. References

1. Rutherford, Phillip R. *A Bibliography of American Doctoral Dissertations in Linguistics,* 1900-1964. Center for Applied Linguistics, Washington, D.C., 1968.
2. *Linguisticinformation.* Center for Applied Linguistics, Washington, D.C., 1965.
3. Cartter, Allan M. "Doctoral Programs in Linguistics," in his *An Assessment of Quality in Graduate Education.* American Council on Education, Washington, D.C., 1966.
4. Various articles on linguistic topics in the *International Encyclopedia of the Social Sciences.* Macmillan, New York, 1968.

Section II

SOME BASIC
SOCIOLINGUISTIC CONCEPTS

Sociolinguistics deals with quite a range of topics: small-group interaction and large-group membership, language use and language attitudes, language-and-behavior norms as well as changes in these norms. We expect to deal with all of these topics, at least briefly, in this section, and necessarily to introduce the technical terms and concepts which specialized fields of discourse inevitably require. However, before moving into any of these more specialized substantive topics there are a number of basic sociolinguistic concepts that are of such general intertopic utility that we had best pause to consider them here, rather than to permit them to remain as primitives any longer.

2.1 LANGUAGE-DIALECT-VARIETY

The term *variety* is frequently utilized in sociolinguistics as a nonjudgmental designation. The very fact that an objective, unemotional, technical term is *needed* in order to refer to "a kind of language" is, in itself, an indication that the expression of "a language" is often a judgmental one, a term that is *indicative* of emotion and opinion, as well as a term that *elicits* emotion and opinion. This is an important fact about languages and one to which we will return repeatedly. As a result, we will use the term "variety" in order not to become trapped in the very phenomena that we seek to investigate, namely, when and by whom is a certain variety considered to be a language and when and by whom is it considered to be something else.

Those varieties that initially and basically represent divergent geographic origins are known as *dialects* (Ferguson and Gumperz 1960; Halliday 1964). It is in this purely objective sense of the word that it is used in such terms as *dialectology* and *dialect geography* within linguistics, and it is in this sense that sociolinguistics employs it as well. However, dialects may easily come to represent (to stand for, to connote, to symbolize) other factors than geographic ones. If immigrants from region A come to be a large portion of the poor, the disliked, and the illiterate in region B, then their speech variety (dialect A) will come to stand for much more than geographic origin alone in the minds of the inhabitants of region B. Dialect A will come to stand for lower social status (educationally, occupationally) than will dialect B. In this way, what was initially a *regional variety* may become a *social variety* or *sociolect* (Blanc 1964). Furthermore, if the speakers of variety A are given hardly any access into the interaction networks of region B, if they marry primarily only each other, engage primarily in their original regional customs, and continue to value only each other's company, they may, in time, come to consider themselves a different society, with goals, beliefs, and traditions of its own. As a result variety A may no longer be viewed as a social variety, but rather as an *ethnic* or *religious* variety and, indeed, it may come to be cultivated as such to the point of being viewed as a separate *language* (Kloss 1967; Fishman 1968c). However, within the community of A speakers there may come to be some who have learned B as well. They may utilize A with each other for purposes of intimacy and in-group solidarity, but they may also use B with each other for occupational and deferential purposes. Thus, for them, A and B will be contrasted and complementary *functional varieties,* with B also being (or including) *a specialized* (occupational) *variety* (Weinreich M. 1953).

The above theoretical sketch has more than general didactic value. It represents the route that many varieties—regional and social—have traveled in the past and the route on which still others are embarked at this very time (Haugen 1966c; Deutsch 1966). Nevertheless, it is the *general* point that is of particular value to us at this juncture. Varieties may be regional at one time and social at another. Varieties may be reacted to as regional within the speech community of their users and as social (or ethnic) by outsiders. Varieties may have additional functional uses for some of their users that they do not have for others who possess fewer contrasted varieties in their verbal repertoires. Thus, the term variety—unlike the term dialect—indicates no particular linguistic status (other than difference) vis-à-vis other varieties. A dialect must be a regional *subunit* in relation to a language, particularly in its vernacular or spoken realization. "Language" is a superordinate designation; "dialect" is a subordinate designation. Both terms require that the entire taxonomy to which they pertain be known before they themselves can be accepted. Sociolinguistics is interested in them only in so far as members of speech communities contend over which is which, and why. As the result of such contention dialects may throw off their subordination and be "promoted" by their speakers to official and independent status, whereas formerly independent languages may become subordinated. The term variety, on the other hand, merely designates a member of a verbal repertoire. Its use implies only that there are other varieties as well. These can be specified by outsiders on the basis of the phonological, lexical, and grammatical differences that they (the varieties) manifest. Their functional allocations, however—as languages or as dialects—are derivable only from societal observation of their uses and users rather than from any characteristics of the codes themselves.

Varieties change over time, but varieties are also *changed,* either by drift or by design. Varieties that have been used in palaces and universities may later come to be used only by the rural and unlettered. In this process their lexicons may well become impoverished, hundreds or thousands of the terms once needed dropping into disuse. At the same time lexicons and grammars as well as phonologies may become much influenced by other temporarily more prestigeful and possibly genetically unrelated varieties. Conversely, varieties that had never been used outside of the most humble speech networks may be elevated in function, increased in lexicon, and purified or enriched in whatever direction their circumstantially improved speakers may desire (Kloss 1952; Fishman 1968c). All varieties of all languages are equally expandable and changeable; all are equally contractable and interpenetrable under the influence of foreign models. Their virtues are in the eyes (or ears) of their beholders. Their functions depend on the norms of the speech communities that employ them. These norms, in turn, change as speech communities change in self-concepts, in their relations with surrounding communities, and in their objective circumstances. Finally, such changes usually lead to changes in the varieties themselves. Speech communities and their varieties are not only interrelated systems; they are completely interdependent systems as well. It is this interdependence that sociolinguistics examines.

2.2 MAJOR TYPES OF ATTITUDE AND BEHAVIOR TOWARD LANGUAGE

One of the best known societal behaviors toward language is *standardization,* i.e., "the codification and acceptance, within a community of users, of a formal set of norms defining 'correct' usage" (Stewart 1968). Codification is, typically, the concern of such language "gatekeepers" as scribes, storytellers, grammarians, teachers, and writers, i.e., of certain groups that arise in most diversified societies and whose use of language is professional and conscious. Codification is formulated and presented to all or part of the speech community via such means as grammars, dictionaries, spellers, style manuals, and exemplary texts, whether written or oral. Finally the acceptance of the formally codified (i.e., the standardized) variety of a language is advanced via such agencies and authorities as the goverment, the educational system, the mass media, etc. The standard variety then becomes associated with these institutions, the types of interactions that most commonly occur within them, and the values or goals they represent (Haugen 1966a).

Note that not all languages have standard varieties. Note also, that where a standard variety does exist it does not necessarily displace the nonstandard varieties from the linguistic repertoires of the speech community for functions that are distinct from but complementary to those of the standard variety. Note, additionally, that there may be several competing standard varieties in the same speech community. Note, finally, that hitherto nonstandard varieties may themselves undergo standardization, whereas hitherto standardized varieties may undergo destandardization as their speakers no longer view them as worthy of codification and cultivation. Standardization is not a property of any language per se, but a characteristic societal treatment of language, given sufficient societal diversity and need for symbolic elaboration.

Another common societal view of language is that which is concerned with its *autonomy,* i.e., with the uniqueness and independence of the linguistic system, or at least of some variety within that system. *Autonomy* is often of little concern to speech communities whose languages differ markedly from each other. These may be said to be autonomous by dint of sheer *abstand* or linguistic distance between them (Kloss 1952; Kloss 1967). On the other hand, where languages seem to be quite similar to each other—phonologically, lexically, and grammatically—it may be of great concern to establish their autonomy from each other, or at least that of the weaker from the stronger. Were such autonomy not to be established it might occur to some that one was "no more than" a dialect (a regional variety) of the other, a subservience which might become part of a rationale for political subservience as well.

A major vehicle of fostering autonomy views concerning a language is its standardization. The availability of dictionaries and grammars is taken as a sure sign that a particular variety is "really a language." However, the availability of dictionaries and grammars not only *represents* autonomy, but also cultivates and increases it by introducing new vocabulary and stressing those phonological and grammatical alternatives that are most different from those of any given autonomy-threatening contrast language. "Heroes are made not born." The same is true of the autonomy of genetically (historically) related languages. Their autonomy has to be worked on. It is not autonomy by *abstand,* but, rather, by *ausbau* (by effort, and often by fiat or decree), and pertains particularly to their standard (and most particularly to their written standard) varieties.

It is a characteristic of the newly rich to supply their own ancestors. In a similar vein those speech communities, the autonomy of whose standard variety is based most completely on *ausbau* activity, are also most likely to be concerned with its *historicity,* that is, with its "respectable" ancestry in times long past. As a result, many speech communities create and cultivate myths and genealogies concerning the origin and development of their standard varieties in order to deemphasize the numerous components of more recent vintage that they contain (Ferguson 1959b). As a result of the widespread preference for *historicity,* currently utilized (and recently liberated or standardized) varieties are found to be derived from ancient prototypes that had largely been forgotten, or are found to be the language of the gods, or to have been created by the same miraculous and mysterious forces and processes that created the speech community itself, etc. Thus, a variety achieves historicity by coming to be associated with some great ideological or national movement or tradition (Fishman 1965c). Usually, historicity provides the ex post facto rationale for functional changes that have occurred with respect to the verbal repertoire of a speech community.

Finally, a speech community's behavior toward any one or another of the varieties in its linguistic repertoire is likely to be determined, at least in part, by the degree to which these varieties have visible *vitality,* i.e., interaction networks that actually employ them natively for one or more vital functions. The more numerous and the more important the native speakers of a particular variety are the greater its vitality and the greater its potential for standardization, autonomy, and historicity. Conversely, the fewer the number and the lower the status of the native speakers of a variety, the more it is reacted to as if it were somehow a defective or contaminated instrument, unworthy of serious efforts or functions, and lacking in proper parentage or uniqueness. As usual, such biased views are likely to be self-fulfilling in that when the numbers and the resources of the users of a given variety dwindle they are less likely to be able to protect its standardization, autonomy, or historicity from the inroads of other speech communities and their verbal repertoires and language-enforcing resources.

Given these four widespread patterns of societal belief and behavior toward language, it is possible to define seven different kinds of varieties, depending upon their absence or presence at any given time (Table 2). Note, however, that any speech community may include in its repertoire a *number of such varieties* which are differentiable on the basis of the four widespread belief-and-behavior systems just discussed. Furthermore, occupational and social class subvarieties are likely to exist within most of the varieties listed in Table 2. In some speech communities deference due an interlocutor with whom one stands in a particular role relationship may be indicated by switching from one social-class variety or from one dialect to another. In other speech communities this very same function may be realized by switching from a

TABLE 2. The Attributes of Different Types of Language Varieties (from Stewart 1968).

*ATTRIBUTES**				*VARIETY-TYPE*	*SYMBOL*
1	2	3	4		
+	+	+	+	Standard	S
−	+	+	+	Vernacular	U
−	−	+	+	Dialect	D
−	−	−	+	Creole	K
−	−	−	−	Pidgin	P
+	+	+	−	Classical	C
+	+	−	−	Artificial	A

*1 = standardization, 2 = autonomy, 3 = historicity, 4 = vitality

dialect to the standard variety (which latter variety, alone, may possess formal verb forms and pronouns of respect). In yet another speech community a switch from one language to another (or from a dialect of one language to the standard variety of another) may be the accepted and recognized realization pattern for deferential interaction. While the precise nature of the switch will depend on the repertoire available to the speech community, switching as such and the differentiae and concepts by means of which it may be noted and explained are of constant interest to sociolinguistic method and theory.

2.3 SPEECH COMMUNITY

Speech community, like variety, is a neutral term. Unlike other societal designations it does not imply any particular size or any particular basis of communality. A speech community is one all of whose members share at least a single speech variety and the norms for its appropriate use. A speech community may be as small as a single closed interaction network, all of whose members regard each other in but a single capacity. Neither of these limitations, however, is typical for speech communities throughout the world and neither is typical for those that have been studied by sociolinguists.

Isolated bands and nomadic clans not only represent small speech communities but speech communities that also exhaust their members' entire network range, while providing little specialization of roles or statuses. Such speech communities usually possess very limited verbal repertoires in terms of different varieties, primarily because one individual's life experiences and responsibilities are pretty much like another's. Nevertheless, such similarity is likely to be more apparent than real. Even small and total societies are likely to differentiate between men and women, between minors and adults, between children and parents, between leaders and followers. Indeed, such societies are likely to have more contact with the "outside world" than is commonly imagined, whether for purposes of trade or exogamy (Owens 1965). Thus, even small total societies reveal functionally differentiated linguistic repertoires (and, not infrequently, intragroup bilingualism as well) based upon behaviorally differentiated interaction networks.

Such small and total (or nearly total) societies differ, of course, from equally small or even smaller family networks, friendship networks, interest networks, or occupational networks within such larger speech communities as tribes, cities, or countries. In the latter cases the interaction networks are not as redundant as in the former (i.e., one more frequently interacts with *different* people in one's various roles as son, friend, work colleague, party member, etc.). However, varieties are needed not only by diverse small networks but also by large networks of individuals who rarely if ever interact, but who have certain interests, views, and allegiances in common. Thus, not only are network redundancy and network size attributes that characterize and differentiate speech communities, but so is the extent to which their existence is experiential rather than merely referential.

One of the characteristics of large and diversified speech communities is that some of the varieties within their verbal repertoires are primarily experientially acquired and reinforced by dint of actual verbal interaction within particular networks, while others are primarily referentially acquired and reinforced by dint of symbolic integration within reference networks which may rarely or never exist in any physical sense. The "nation" or the "region" are likely to constitute a speech community of this latter type, and the standard ("national") language or the regional language is likely to represent its corresponding linguistic variety.

Many American cities present ample evidence of both of these bases—verbal interaction and symbolic integration—for the functioning of speech communities. Every day hundreds of thousands of residents of Connecticut, upstate New York, and various parts of Pennsylvania come to New York City to work and shop. In terms of waking hours of actual face-to-face verbal interaction these speakers of dialects that differ from New York City English may talk more, and more frequently, to New Yorkers than they do to inhabitants of their places of residence and to speakers of their local dialects. How then can we explain the fact that not only do most of them differentially utilize the markers of their local dialects (and not only during the evenings, weekends, and holidays, when they are at home rather than at work), but the simultaneous fact that many of them can and do also employ a more regionally neutral variety, which is their approximation to "Standard American," as distinct from New York City English on the one hand and Lower Connecticut Village English on the other? Obviously, the "Standard American" of these commuters to New York City cannot be based on much verbal interaction with a separate network known as "the American people," nor can it be based upon any other interaction network, however referred to, whose speakers use "Standard American" and it alone. There is no other alternative but to conclude that the speech community of "Standard American" represents a reference group for the denizens of Connecticut villages, while "Standard American" itself is a variety that has the functions of "symbolic integration with the nation" in their linguistic repertoire.

Thus, some speech communities and their linguistic repertoires are preserved primarily by communication gaps that separate them from other communities and their repertoires. Other speech communities and their repertoires are preserved primarily by the force of symbolic (attitudinal) integration even in the absence of face-to-face interaction. Many speech communities contain networks of both types. Many networks contain both kinds of members. Societal norms that define communicative appropriateness can apply with equal force and regularity regardless of whether direct interaction or symbolic integration underlies their implementation.

As mentioned earlier, the standard variety of a language is most likely to be that variety that stands for the nation as a whole and for its most exalted institutions of government, education, and high culture in general. It is this variety which comes to be associated with the mission, glory, history, and uniqueness of an entire "people" and, indeed, it is this variety which helps unite individuals who do not otherwise constitute an interaction network into a symbolic speech community or "people." Thus it is that standard varieties and larger-than-face-to-face speech communities are historically and functionally interdependent. While interaction networks of speakers of standard varieties doubtlessly do exist (literati, scholars, social and educational elites, etc.), these are likely to arrive at somewhat specialized usages, on the one hand, as well as to require a nonstandard variety, on the other hand, if they are to engage in more intimate and informal kinds of interactions as well. Thus, the standard language per se, without further differentiation or accompaniment, is most fitted for communication across large but nonexistent (or noninteracting) networks, such as those involving the mass media, governmental pronouncements, legal codes, and textbooks.

The standard variety is the "safest" for those communications in which a speaker cannot know his diversified and numerous listeners (Joos 1959). However, the more the communication is expected to live on over an appreciable period of time, independently of both speaker and listener (or sender and receiver), the more it will be viewed as archaic (or classical) rather than merely "standard."

A basic definitional property of speech communities is that they are *not* defined as communities of those who "speak the same language" (notwithstanding Bloomfield 1933), but rather as communities set off by density of communication or/and by symbolic integration with respect to communicative competence *regardless of the number of languages or varieties employed* (Gumperz 1964a). The complexity of speech communities thus defined will vary with the extent of variation in the experiential and attitudinal networks which they subsume. Speech communities can be so selected as to include greater or lesser diversity on each of these grounds. In general the verbal repertoire of a speech community is a reflection of its role repertoire (in terms of both implemented and ideologized roles). This reflection pertains not only to repertoire *range* but also to repertoire *access* and *fluidity*.

Speech communities with a larger role repertoire reveal a larger verbal repertoire as well (Gumperz 1962). Communities most of whose members are alike in daily experiences and in life aspirations will also tend to show little linguistic range in terms of differentiable varieties. This tends to be the case not only in the small, total communities that were mentioned earlier but also, some suspect, in large, democratic, industrialized communities of the most modern sort. Actually, both kinds of speech communities show more repertoire range (in terms of verbal repertoire and in terms of role repertoire) than is obvious on superficial inspection. Nevertheless, they both tend to have narrower (and less diversified) ranges than are encountered in the stratified speech communities that exist in intermediate societies of the traditional, non-Western World. Whereas the modern, open speech community tends to reveal several varieties of the same language, the more traditional speech community will typically reveal varieties of several languages (see Figure 1).

These two types of speech communities are also quite likely to differ in the extent to which their members have *access* to the roles and to the varieties available in the respective repertoires of their communities. In the more traditional speech communities access to certain roles is severely restricted and is attained, in those cases in which access to new roles *is* available, on the basis of *ascription.* Those whose ancestry is inappropriate cannot attain certain new roles, regardless of their personal achievement. Similarly, access to an expanded verbal repertoire is also severely restricted, most

FIGURE 1. *Speech Communities and Verbal Repertoires* (based upon concepts of Gumperz 1964a and elsewhere)

Societal Domain	Speech Community 1	Speech Community 2	Speech Community 3	Speech Community 4
Home	a_1	c_1	c_1	d_1
School and Culture	a_2	c_2	b_2	a_2
Work	a_3	c_3	d_2	d_2
Government	a_2	b_1	a_2	a_2
Church	e_1	b_2	b_2	e_1
	(Moscow, 1960) [Russians]	(Mea Shearim, 1966) [Jews]	(Ostropol, 1905) [Jews]	(Ostropol, 1905) [Ukrainians]

Some communities have more obviously diversified repertoires than others (e.g., SC*1* utilized three varieties of one language and one of another, whereas SC*3* utilized varieties of four different languages). Varieties that are related to one societal domain in one SC (e.g., b_2 in SC*2*) may be associated with more or different societal domains in another SC (e.g., b_2 in SC*3*). All speakers of varieties of a particular language do not necessarily constitute a single speech community.

varieties not learned in childhood being available only to those who can afford to devote many years of patient and painstaking formal study to their acquisition. Both of these conditions are not nearly so likely to exist in modern, personal-achievement-oriented societies, although their lack of completely equal and open access is evident to all students of the disadvantaged (including Negro nonstandard speech) in the midst of America's plenty.

In more traditional societies in which status is based on ascription there is also likely to be more role *compartmentalization*. Thus, not only are certain individuals barred from enacting certain roles, but in general the rights and duties that constitute particular roles are more distinct and the transitions from one role to the next, for members of those classes who may enter into them, are ritually governed, as are the roles themselves. Such societies also tend to reveal marked verbal compartmentalization as well (McCormack 1962). When an individual speaks language or variety A he takes great care not to switch into B and not to slip into traces of B, whether phonologically, lexcally, or grammatically. Each variety is kept separate and uncontaminated from the other just as is each role. How different such compartmentalization is from the fluidity of modern democratic speech communities in which there is such frequent change from one role to another and from one variety to another that individuals are frequently father and pal or teacher and colleague simultaneously or in rapid succession! The result of such frequent and easy role shifts is often that the roles themselves become more similar and less distinctive or clearcut. The same occurs in the verbal repertoire as speakers change from one variety (or language) to another with greater frequency and fluidity. The varieties too tend to become more similar as the roles in which they are appropriate become more and more alike. This is particularly likely to occur, as we shall see below, among lower-class speakers whose mastery of the more formal roles and varieties available to their speech communities is likely to be marginal at best.

Thus, just as varieties are characterizable by a small number of attributes and their combinations, so is this true of the attributes that characterize speech communities at the most general level. The interactional basis of speech communities, their symbolic-integrative basis, their size, repertoire range, repertoire access, and repertoire compartmentalization are all concepts that we shall need to refer to again and again in the pages that follow.

Section III

INTERACTIONAL SOCIOLINGUISTICS: MICRO AND MACRO

Boss	Carmen, do you have a minute?
Secretary	Yes, Mr. Gonzalez.
Boss	I have a letter to dictate to you.
Secretary	Fine. Let me get my pen and pad. I'll be right back.
Boss	Okay.
Secretary	Okay.
Boss	Okay, this is addressed to Mr. William Bolger.
Secretary	That's B-o-r-g-e-r?
Boss	B-o-l
Secretary	Oh, oh, I see.
Boss	Okay. His address is in the files.
Secretary	Okay.
Boss	Okay. Dear Bill, Many thanks for telling me about your work with the Science Research Project. The information you gave me ought to prove most helpful.
Secretary	That was "The information you gave me ought to prove most helpful."

Boss   Correct.

Secretary   Okay.

Boss   Okay, ah. I very much appreciate the time you gave me. Never mind, strike that out. Ah, enclosed are two of the forms that you let me borrow. I'll be sending back the data sheets very soon. Thanks again, I hope that your hospital stay will be as pleasant as possible and that your back will be soon in top shape. Will soon be in top shape. It was nice seeing you again. Sincerely, Louis Gonzalez

Secretary   Do you have the enclosures for the letter, Mr. Gonzalez?

Boss   Oh yes, here they are.

Secretary   Okay.

Boss   Ah, this man William Bolger got his organization to contribute a lot of money to the Puerto Rican parade. He's very much for it.

             ¿Tú fuiste a la parada?
             (Did you go to the parade?)

Secretary   Sí, yo fuí.
             (Yes, I went.)

Boss   ¿Sí?
             (Yes?)

Secretary   Uh huh.

Boss   ¿Y cómo te estuvo?
             (And how did you like it?)

Secretary   Ay, lo más bonita.
             (Oh, very pretty.)

Boss   Sí, porque yo fuí y yo nunca había participado en la parada y
             (Yes, because I went and I had never participated in the parade and

este año me dió curiosidad por ir a ver como
era y estuvo eso

this year I became curious to go and see how it
was and that was

fenómeno. Fuí con mi señora y con mis nenes y
a ellos también

a phenomenon. I went with my wife and my
children and they

le gustó mucho. Eh, y tuve día bien agradable.
Ahora lo que

also liked it very much. And I had a pleasant
day. Now

me molesta a mi es que las personas cuando
viene una cosa así,

what bothers me is that people when something
like this comes along,

la parada Puertorriqueña o la fiesta de San Juan,
corren de la

the Puerto Rican parade, or the festival of San
Juan they run from

casa a participar porque es una actividad festiva,
alegre, y sin

the house to participate because it is a festive
activity, happy, and

embargo, cuando tienen que ir a la iglesia, o la
misa para pedirle . . .

then, when they have to go to church or to
mass, to ask . . .

Secretary	(Laughter)
Boss	A Diós entonce no van.
	(God then they don't go.)
Secretary	Sí, entonces no van.
	(Yes, then they don't go.)

Boss   Pero, así es la vida, caramba. Do you think that
            you could get
            (But that's life, you know.)
            this letter out today?

Secretary   Oh yes, I'll have it this afternoon for you.

Boss   Okay, good, fine then.

Secretary   Okay.

Boss   Okay.

If we carefully consider the above conversation it becomes evident that it reveals considerable internal variation. Speaker A does not always speak in the same way nor does his interlocutor, Speaker B. Were it possible for us to listen to the original tapes of this conversation, several *kinds* of variation within each of them would become evident to us: variations in speed of speaking, variations in the extent to which Spanish phonology creeps into English discourse and vice versa, variations in the extent to which English phonology creeps into the Spanish discourse, etc. However, even from the conventionally (orthographically) rendered transcription available to us on the previous pages one kind of variation remains exceedingly clear: that from Spanish to English or from English to Spanish for each speaker. It is precisely because bilingual code switching is often more noticeable than other kinds of sociolinguistic variation that bilingualism is so commonly examined in sociolinguistic theory and research. However, the concepts and findings that derive from such examinations must be provocative and illuminating for sociolinguistics more generally. And, indeed, that *is* the case, for the societal patterning of bilingual interaction is merely an instance (hopefully, a more obvious and, therefore, pedagogically useful instance) of the vastly more general phenomenon of societal patterning of variation in verbal interaction.

How shall we describe or measure the phenomenon of interest to us: societal patterning of variation in verbal interaction? Usefully accurate description or measurement is certainly the basic problem of every scientific field of endeavor. Most of mankind has constantly been immersed in a veritable ocean of crosscurrents of talk. Nevertheless, as with most other aspects of everyday social behavior, it is only in very recent days that man has begun to recognize the latent order and regularity in the manifest chaos of verbal interaction that surrounds him.

3.1 HOW SHOULD TALK BE CONTEXTUALLY DESCRIBED?

How should "talk" be contextually described in order to best reveal or discover its social systemization (assuming that its "basic" linguistic description is already available)? Let us begin with some passages of actual "talk," making sure to preserve its verbatim form (preferably, by utilizing sensitive audio and visual recording equipment) rather than merely summarizing the content of such talk. The smallest sociolinguistic unit that will be of interest to us is a *speech act:* a joke, an interjection, an opening remark (Schegloff 1968a), a question, in general—a segment of talk that is also societally recognizable and reoccurring. Speech acts are normally parts of somewhat larger *speech events,* such as conversations, introductions, lectures, prayers, arguments, etc. (Hymes 1967), which, of course, must also be societally recognizable and reoccurring.

If we note that a switch has occurred from variety a to variety b—perhaps from a kind of Spanish to a kind of English, or from more formal English to less formal English, or from regionally neutral, informal Spanish to Jíbaro (rural) informal Spanish—the first question that presents itself is whether one variety tends to be used (or used more often) in certain kinds of speech acts or events whereas the other tends to be used (or used more often) in others. Thus, were we aware of the speech acts recognized by bilingual Puerto Rican youngsters in New York, we might venture to explain a switch such as the following:

First Girl	Yes, and don't tell me that the United States is the only one that has been able to in Puerto Rico. . . .
Boy	Okay so you have a couple of people like Moscoso and Luís Ferrer.
First Girl	¡ Un momento!
Boy	¡ Bueno!
First Girl	¡ Un momento!
Boy	Have you got people capable of starting something like . . . like General Motors?

as being related to the act of interruption or disagreement in the midst of a somewhat specialized argument. There may be a problem, however, when testing this interpretation, in determining the speech acts and speech events that are to be recognized within a speech community.

Certainly, it is not appropriate to simply apply the system of acts and events that has been determined for one speech community in the study of another, without first determining its appropriateness in the second community. Similarly, it is not sufficient for the investigator, no matter how much experience he has had with the verbal behavior of a particular speech community, merely to devise as detailed a listing of speech acts and events as he can. Such a list runs the decided risk of being *etic* rather than *emic,* i.e., of making far too many, as well as behaviorally inconsequential, differentiations, just as was often the case with phon*etic* vs. phon*emic* analysis in linguistics proper. An *emic* set of speech acts and events must be one that is validated as meaningful via final recourse to the native members of a speech community rather than via appeal to the investigator's ingenuity or intuition alone.

An *emic* set of speech acts and speech events is best approximated, perhaps along a never-ending asymptote, by playing back recorded samples of "talk" to native speakers and by encouraging them to react to and comment upon the reasons for the use of variety *a* "here" as contrasted with the use of variety *b* "there." The more the sensitive investigator observes the speech community that he seeks to describe sociolinguistically the more hunches he will have concerning functionally different speech acts and speech events. However, even the best hunches require verification *from within the speech community.* Such verification may take various shapes. The views of both naïve and skilled informants may be cited and tabulated as they comment upon recorded instances of variation in "talk" and as they reply to the investigator's patient probes and queries as to "Why didn't he say 'Just a minute!' instead of '¡Momento!'? Would it have meant something different if he *had* said that instead? When is it appropriate to say '¡Momento!' and when is it appropriate to say 'Just a minute!' (assuming the persons involved know both languages equally well)?", etc. Once the investigator has *demonstrated* (not merely assumed or argued) the validity of his sets of functionally different speech acts and events, he may then proceed to utilize them in the collection and analysis of samples of talk which are *independent* of those already utilized for validational purposes. Such, at least, is the rationale of research procedure at this microlevel of sociolinguistic analysis, although the field itself is still too young and too linguistically oriented to have produced many instances of such cross-validation of its *social* units selected for purposes of *socio*linguistic analysis.

3.2 MICROLEVEL ANALYSIS IN SOCIOLINGUISTICS

Sociolinguistic description may merely begin—rather than end—with the specification and the utilization of speech acts and events, depending on the purpose of a particular research enterprise. The more linguistically oriented a particular study may be, the more likely it is to remain content with microlevel analysis, since the microlevel in sociolinguistics is already a much higher (i.e., a more contextual and complicated) level of analysis than that traditionally employed within linguistics proper. However, the more societally oriented a particular sociolinguistic study may be, the more concerned with investigating social processes and societal organization per se, the more likely it is to seek successively more macro-level analyses. Microlevel sociolinguistics (sometimes referred to as ethnomethodological sociolinguistics) constitutes one of the levels within sociolinguistic inquiry (Garfinkel 1967; Garfinkel and Sacks 1968). The various levels do not differ in the degree to which they are correct or accurate. They differ in purpose and therefore in method. We can trace only a few of the successive levels in this section, primarily in order to demonstrate their similarities and their differences.

One of the awarenesses to which an investigator may come after pondering a mountain of sociolinguistic data at the level of speech acts and events is that variation in "talk" is more common and differently proportioned or distributed between certain interlocutors than it is between others (Schegloff 1968a, 1968b). Thus, whereas either the boy or the girl in Conversation 2 may initiate the switch from one language to another, it may seem from Conversation 1 that the boss is the initiator of switching far more frequently than is the secretary. Therefore, while a great deal of switching is functionally *metaphorical,* i.e., it indicates a contrast in emphasis (from humor to seriousness, from agreement to disagreement, from the inessential or secondary to the essential or primary, in any interchange already underway in a particular language variety), interlocutors may vary in the extent to which they may appropriately initiate or engage in such switching, depending on their *role relationships* to each other. Note, however, that it is necessary for a certain appropriateness to exist between a variety and certain characteristics of the social setting before it is possible to utilize another variety for metaphorical or contrastive purposes.

3.3 ROLE RELATIONSHIPS

Any two interlocutors within a given speech community (or, more narrowly, within a given speech network within a speech community) must recognize the role relationship that exists between them at any particular time. Such recognition is part of the communality of norms and behaviors upon which the existence of speech communities depends. Father-son, husband-wife, teacher-pupil, clergyman-layman, employer-employee, friend-friend: these are but some examples of the role relationships that may exist in various (but not in all) speech communities (Goodenough 1965). Role relationships are implicitly recognized and accepted sets of mutual rights and obligations between members of the same sociocultural system. One of the ways in which members reveal such common membership to each other, as well as their recognition of the rights and obligations that they owe toward each other, is via appropriate variation (which, of course, may include appropriate nonvariation) of the way(s) they talk to each other. Perhaps children should generally be seen and not heard, but when they *are* heard most societies insist that they talk differently to their parents than they do to their friends (Fischer 1958). One of the frequent comments about American travelers abroad is that they know (*at most*) only one variety of the language of the country they are visiting. As a result, they speak in the same way to a child, a professor, a bootblack, and a shopkeeper, thus revealing not only their foreignness, but also their ignorance of the appropriate ways of signaling local role relationships.

It is probably not necessary, at this point, to dwell upon the kinds of variation in talk that may be required (or prohibited) by certain role relationships. In addition, and this too should require no extensive discussion at this point, whether the variation required is from one language to another or from one geographic, social, or occupational variety to another, the functionally differential role relationships must be *emically* validated rather than merely *etically* enumerated. There are certainly sociolinguistic allo-roles in most speech communities. However, two other characterizations of role relationships do merit mention at this point, particularly because they have proved to be useful in sociolinguistic description and analysis.

Role relationships vary in the extent to which their mutual rights and obligations must or must not be *continually stressed.* The king-subject role relationship may retain more invariant steps than the shopkeeper-customer relationship. If shopkeepers and their customers may also interact with each other as friends, as relatives, as members of the same political party, etc., whereas kings and their subjects (in the same speech community) may not experience a similar degree of role range, access, and fluidity *vis-à-vis each other,* then we would expect to encounter more variation in the "talk" of two individuals who encounter each other as shopkeeper and customer than we would expect between two individuals who encounter each other as king and subject. In addition, a shopkeeper and his customer may be able to set aside their roles entirely and interact entirely on the basis of their individual and momentary needs and inclinations. This may not be permissible for the king and his subjects. Thus, we should say that a shopkeeper and his customer may engage in both *personal* and *transactional* interactions (Gumperz 1964a), whereas the king and his subjects engage only in transactional interactions. Transactional interactions are those which stress the mutual rights and obligations of their participants. Personal interactions are more informal, more fluid, more varied.

In part, speech acts and events are differentially distributed throughout various role relationships because personal and transactional interactions are differentially permitted in various role relationships. Sociolinguistics is necessarily of interest to those investigators who are concerned with determining the functionally different role relationships that exist within a given community. Microsociolinguistics, at least, is concerned with the validation of such relationships, via the demonstration of differential role access, role range, and role fluidity, as well as via the demonstration of differential proportions of personal and transactional interaction, through the data of "talk." Role relationships may be used as data-organizing units both with respect to variation in talk as well as with respect to other variations in interpersonal behavior.

This is the reason why role relations are so frequently examined in sociolinguistics.

3.4 THE SITUATION: CONGRUENT AND INCONGRUENT

It has probably occurred to the reader that if the shopkeeper and his customer are not to interact only as such, but rather also as friends, lovers, relatives, or party members, that more than their roles are likely to change. After all, neither the *time* nor the *place* of the storekeeper-customer role relationship is really ideal for any of the other relationships mentioned. Lovers require a time and a place of their own, and the same is true—or, at least, is typical—for other role relationships as well. These three ingredients (the *implementation* of the rights and duties of a particular role relationship, in the *place* (locale) most appropriate or most typical for that relationship, and at the *time* societally defined as appropriate for that relationship), taken together, constitute a construct that has proven itself to be of great value in sociolinguistics: the *social situation* (Bock 1964; see Tables 3 and 4).

The simplest type of social situation for microsociolinguistics to describe and analyze is the congruent situation in which all three ingredients "go-together" in the culturally expected way. This is not to say that the investigator may assume that there is only one place and one time appropriate for the realization of a particular role relationship. Quite the contrary. As with the wakes studied by Bock on a Micmac Indian Reserve, there may be various times and various places for the appropriate realization of particular role relationships

TABLE 3. *The Social Situation* (Bock 1964).

SITUATION: "CLASS"		*Time:* Class Meeting
Space: Classroom		*Roles:* + Teacher + Pupil ± Student-Teacher

+ indicates obligatory occurrence
± indicates optional occurrence

TABLE 4. Situation-Matrix #14: Indian Wake (Bock, 1964).

M-14			T-1	T-2	T-3	T-4	T-5
S-1: Bier	s-1.1: nucleus		R-1	R-1	R-1	R-1	R-1
Area	s-1.2: margin		±R-2			±R-2	
S-2: Front Area				R-3	R-4		r-2.1
S-3: Audience Area				R-2	R-2	±R-2 ±R-4	r-2.2 R-4
S-4: Mar-ginal	s-4.1: kitchen					r-2.1	
Area	s-4.2: outside		r-2.2			±r-2.2 ±R-4	

14. SC-A: Place of Wake—External distribution into 9.S-A.1: House site (usually that occupied by deceased).

S-1:   Bier Area

s-1.1:   nuclus—contains coffin

s-1.2:   margin—area immediately surrounding coffin

S-2:   Front Area—focal region of performances during T-2, -3, and -5.

S-3:   Audience Area—seating area for R-2: Mourner

S-4:   Marginal Area—residual space, including

s-4.1:   kitchen area

s-4.2:   outside of house

14. TC-A: Time of Wake—External distribution (see discussion above).
TC-A = //T-1/T-2//:T-3/T-4://±T-5//:T-3/T-4://

T-1:   Gathering Time—participants arrive at SC-A: Place of Wake

T-2:   Prayer Time—saying of the Rosary by R-3: Prayer Leader

T-3:   Singing Time—several hymns sung with brief pauses in between

T-4:   Intermission—longer pause in singing

T-5:   Meal Time—optional serving of meal (about midnight)

14. RC-A: Participant Roles—External distribution noted for each:

R-1:   Corpse—from 3: RC-A: Band Member

R-2:   Mourner

r-2.1:   Host—member of 9.RC-A: Household Group (of deceased)

r-2.2:   Other—residual category

R-3:   Prayer Leader

r-3.1:   Priest—from 3.R-B.1.1: Priest

r-3.2:   Other—from 14.R-4

R-4:   Singer—usually from 11.R-A.4: Choir Member

(see Table 4). Nevertheless, the total number of permissible combinations is likely to be small and small or not, there is likely to be little ambiguity among members of the society or culture under study as to what the situation in question is and what its requirements are with respect to their participation in it. As a result, if there are language usage norms with respect to situations these are likely to be most clearly and uniformly realized in avowedly congruent situations.

However, lovers quarrel. Although they meet in the proper time and place, they do not invariably behave toward each other as lovers should. Similarly, if a secretary and a boss are required to meet in the office at 3:00 A.M. in order to complete an emergency report, it may well be difficult for them to maintain the usual secretary-boss relationship. Finally, if priest and parishioner meet at the Yonkers Raceway during the time normally set aside for confessions, this must have some impact on the normal priest-parishioner role relationship. However, in all such instances of initial incongruency (wrong behavior, wrong time, or wrong place) the resulting interaction—whether sociolinguistic or otherwise—is normally far from random or chaotic. One party to the interaction of another, if not both, reinterprets the seeming incongruency so as to yield a congruent situation, at least phenomenologically, for that particular encounter, where one does not exist socioculturally.

Because of incongruent behavior toward each other lovers may reinterpret each other as employer and employee and the date situation is reinterpreted as a dispassionate work situation. Because of the incongruent time, secretary and boss may view the work situation as more akin to a date than is their usual custom. Because of the incongruent place priest and parishioner may pretend not to recognize each other, or to treat each other as "old pals." In short, after a bit of fumbling around, in which various and varying tentative redefinitions may be tried out, a new congruent situation is interpreted as existing and *its* behavioral and sociolinguistic requirements are implemented (Blom and Gumperz 1968;

Fishman 1968b). Thus, whereas bilingual Puerto Rican parents and their children in New York are most likely to talk to each other in Spanish at home when conversing about family matters, they will probably speak in English to each other in the public school building (Fishman, Cooper, and Ma 1968). As far as they are concerned these are two different situations, perhaps calling for two different role relationships and requiring the utilization of two different languages or varieties.

Situational contrasts need not be as discontinuous as most of our examples have thus far implied. Within a basically Spanish-speaking situation one or another member of a bilingual speech community may still switch to English (or, in Paraguay, to Guaraní) in the midst of a speech event for purely metaphorical purposes. Such *metaphorical* purposes could not be served, however, if there were no general norm assigning the particular situation, as one of a class of such situations, to one language rather than to the other. However, in contrast to the largely unilateral and fluid back-and-forth nature of metaphorical switching (perhaps to indicate a personal interlude in a basically transactional interaction) there stands the more reciprocal and unidirectional nature of *situational* switching. In the midst of a discussion the interlocutors recognize an intense dislike for each other (or go over from talking about baseball to talking about electrical engineering) and both quickly change the variety of "talk" that is employed. When friends come to view each other as nonfriends, when mountain climbers pass beyond a certain altitude and relative safety, when officers and their men find themselves in an unexpected danger, it is only natural that this situational change be evident in their sociolinguistic usage. What has changed is far more than the topic of conversation (the latter being part and parcel of appropriate role behavior to begin with). What has changed is the definition of the situation in which the interlocutors find themselves.

3.5 THE TRANSITION TO MACRO - SOCIOLINGUISTICS

The situational analysis of language and behavior represents the boundary area between micro- and macrosociolinguistics. The very fact that a baseball conversation "belongs" to one speech variety and an electrical engineering lecture "belongs" to another speech variety is a major key to an even more generalized description of sociolinguistic variation. The very fact that humor during a formal lecture is realized through a metaphorical switch to another variety must be indicative of an underlying sociolinguistic regularity, perhaps of the view that lecturelike or formal situations are generally associated with one language or variety whereas levity or intimacy is tied to another (Joos 1959). The large-scale aggregative regularities that obtain between varieties and societally recognized functions are examined via the construct termed *domain* (Fishman 1965d; Fishman 1970).

Sociolinguistic domains are societal constructs derived from painstaking analysis and summarization of patently congruent situations (see Fishman, Cooper, and Ma 1968, for many examples of the extraction of *emic* domains via factor analysis as well as for examples of the validation of initially *etic* domains). The macrosociologist or social psychologist may well inquire: What is the significance of the fact that school situations and "schoolish" situations (the latter being initially incongruent situations reinterpreted in the direction of their most salient component) are related to variety *a*? Frequently, it is helpful to recognize a number of behaviorally separate domains (behaviorally separate in that they are derived from discontinuous social situations), all of which are commonly associated with a particular variety or language. Thus, in many bilingual speech communities such domains as school, church, professional work sphere, and government have been verified and found to be congruent with a language or variety that we will refer to as H (although for purely labeling purposes we might refer to it as *a* or X or 1). Similarly, such domains as family, neighborhood, and lower work sphere have been validated and found to be congruent with a language or variety that we will refer to as L (or *b,* or Y or 2). All in all, the fact that a complex speech community contains various superposed varieties—in some cases, various languages, and in others, various varieties of the same language—is now well documented. The existence of complementary varieties for intragroup purposes is known as *diglossia* (Ferguson 1959a) and the communities in which diglossia is encountered are referred to as *diglossic.* Domains are particularly useful constructs for the macrolevel (i.e., community-wide) functional description of societally patterned variation in "talk" within large and complex diglossic speech communities, about which more will be said in Section Six.

Some members of diglossic speech communities can verbalize the relationship between certain broad categories of behavior and certain broad categories of "talk." More educated and verbally fluent members of speech communities can tell an investigator about such relationships at great length and in great detail. Less educated and verbally limited members can only grope to express a regularity which they vaguely realize exists. However, the fact that the formulation of a regular association between language (variety) and large-scale situational behaviors may be difficult to come by is no more indicative of a dubious relationship than the fact that grammatical regularities can rarely be explicitly formulated by native speakers is to be considered as calling the abstracted rules themselves into question.

As with all constructs (including situations, role relationships, and speech events), domains originate in the integrative intuition of the investigator. If the investigator notes that student-teacher interactions in classrooms, school corridors, school auditoriums, and school laboratories of elementary schools, high schools, colleges, and universities are all realized via H as long as these interactions are focused upon educational technicality and specialization, he may begin to suspect that these hypothetically congruent situations all belong to a single (educational) *domain.* If he further finds that hypothetically incongruent situations involving an educational and a noneducational ingredient are, by and large, predictably resolved in terms of H rather than L if the third ingredient is an educational time, place, or role relationship, he may feel further justified in positing an educational domain. Finally, if informants tell him that the predicted language or variety would be appropriate in all of the examples he can think of that derive from his notion of the educational domain, whereas they proclaim that it would not be appropriate for examples that he draws from a contrasted domain, then the construct is as usefully validated as is that of situation or event—with one major difference.

Whereas particular speech acts (and speech excerpts of an even briefer nature) can be apportioned to the speech events and social situations in which they occurred, the same cannot be done with respect to such acts or excerpts in relationship to societal domains. Domains are extrapolated from the *data* of "talk" rather than being an actual component of the *process* of talk. However, domains are as real as the very social institutions of a speech community, and indeed they show a marked paralleling with such major social institutions (Barker 1947). There is an undeniable difference between the social institution, "the family," and any particular family, but there is no doubt that the societal norms concerning the former must be derived from data on many instances of the latter. Once such societal norms are formulated they can be utilized to test predictions concerning the distributions of societally patterned variation in talk across all instances of one domain vs. all instances of another.

Thus domains and social situations reveal the links that exist between micro- and macrosociolinguistics. The members of diglossic speech communities can come to have certain views concerning their varieties or languages because these varieties are associated (in behavior and in attitude) with particular domains. The H variety (or language) is considered to reflect certain values and relationships within the speech community, whereas the L variety is considered to reflect others. Certain individuals and groups may come to advocate the expansion of the functions of L into additional domains. Others may advocate the displacement of L entirely and the use of H solely. Neither of these revisionist views could be held or advocated without recognition of the reality of domains of language-and-behavior in terms of *existing* norms of communicative appropriateness. The high-culture values with which certain varieties are associated and the intimacy and folksiness values with which others are congruent are both derivable from domain-appropriate norms governing characteristic verbal interaction.

3.6 SOCIOLINGUISTICS: MULTILEVEL AND MULTIMETHOD

The list of constructs utilized in the sociolinguistic description and analysis of samples of "talk" is far from exhausted. We have not mentioned several of the social units long advocated by Hymes (1962) such as the participant vs. audience roles, the purposes and the outcomes of speech events, the tone or manner of communication, the channel of communication employed (oral, written, telegraphic), nor have we mentioned the social or educational class of interlocutors (Ross 1965), or the saliency of individual vs. collective needs (Herman 1961), etc., etc. Suffice it to say that there are several levels and approaches to sociolinguistic description and a host of linguistic, sociolinguistic, and societal constructs within each (see Figure 2). The choice among them depends on the particular problem at hand (Ervin-Tripp 1964). This is necessarily so. Sociolinguistics is of interest to students of small societies as well as to students of national and international integration. It must help clarify the change from one face-to-face situation to another. It must also help clarify the different language-related beliefs and behaviors of entire social sectors and classes. In some cases the variation between closely related varieties must be highlighted. In

FIGURE 2. Relationships among Some Constructs Employed in Socio-linguistic Analysis*

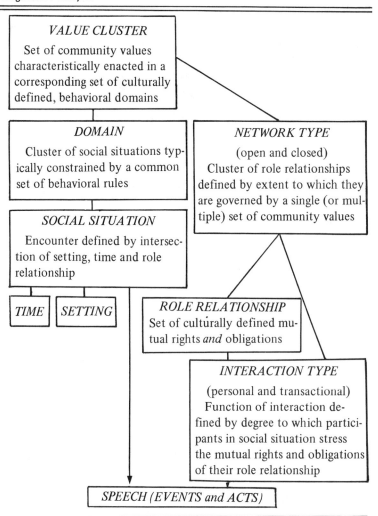

*From Robert L. Cooper. How Can We Measure The Roles Which A Bilingual's Languages Play in His Everyday Behavior? *Preprints* of The International Seminar on the Measurement and Description of Bilingualism. Ottawa, Canadian Commission for Unesco, (1967), pp. 119-132.

other cases the variation between obviously unrelated languages is of concern.

It would be foolhardy to demand that one and the same method of data collection and data analysis be utilized for such a variety of problems and purposes. It is one of the hallmarks of scientific social inquiry that methods are selected as a *result* of problem specifications rather than independently of them. Sociolinguistics is neither methodologically nor theoretically uniform. Nevertheless, it is gratifying to note that for those who seek such ties the links between micro- and macroconstructs and methods exist (as do a number of constructs and methods that have wide applicability through the entire range of sociolinguistics). Just as there is no societally unencumbered verbal interaction, so are there no large scale relationships between language and society that do not depend on individual interaction for their realization. Although there is no mechanical part-whole relationship between them, micro- and macrosociolinguistics are both conceptually and methodologically complementary.

Section IV

SOCIETAL DIFFERENTIATION AND REPERTOIRE RANGE

Speech communities—particularly those at the city-wide, regional, or national levels—obviously vary in the degrees and kinds of language diversity that they reveal. What do such differences imply with respect to the social differentiation and organization of the communities and networks to which they apply? If we examine the varieties of Javanese required by linguistic etiquette in the communities described by Geertz (1960), the varieties of Baghdadi Arabic described by Blanc (1964), the varieties of Hindi or Kannada described by Gumperz (1958) or McCormack (1960), and the varieties of Indonesian described by Tanner (1967), it is clear that these compose quite different kinds of repertoires than do the varieties of Norwegian described by Haugen (1961) or the varieties of American English described by Labov (1963, 1964, 1965) or by Levine and Crockett (1966). In addition, the types of speech communities in which these varieties are encountered also differ strikingly, as do the larger national or regional units in which the communities are embedded. To put it very briefly, the speech communities in the first cluster seem to be much more stratified socially and to employ much more diversified repertoires linguistically than do those in the second. The document co-occurrence of linguistic

TABLE 5A. Dialect of Non-Prijaji, Urbanized, Somewhat Educated Persons.

Level	are	you	going	to eat	rice	and	cassava	now	Complete sentence
3a	menapa	pandjenengan	badé	dahar	sekul	kalijan	kaspé	samenika	*Menapa pandjenengan badé dahar sekul kalijan kaspé samenika?*
3	menapa	pandjenengan	badé	neda	sekul	kalijan	kaspé	samenika	*Menapa sampéjan badé neda sekul kalijan kaspé samenika?*
2	napa	sampéjan	adjeng	neda	sekul	lan	kaspé	saniki	*Napa sampéjan adjeng neda sekul lan kaspé saniki?*
1a	apa	sampéjan	arep	neda	sega	lan	kaspé	saiki	*Apa sampéjan arep neda sega lan kaspé saiki?*
1	apa	kowé	arep	mangan	sega	lan	kaspé	saiki	*Apa kowé arep mangan sega lan kaspé saiki?*

TABLE 5B. Dialect of Peasants and Uneducated Townspeople.

Level	are	you	going	to eat	rice	and	cassava	now	Complete sentence
2	napa	sampéjan	adjeng	neda	sekul	lan	kaspé	saniki	*Napa sampéjan adjeng neda sekul lan kaspé saniki?*
1a	apa	sampéjan	arep	neda	sega	lan	kaspé	saiki	*Apa sampéjan arep neda sega lan kaspé saiki?*
1	apa	kowé	arep	mangan	sega	lan	kaspé	saiki	*Apa kowé arep mangan sega lan kaspé saiki?*

TABLE 5C. Dialect of the Prijajis.

Level	are	you	going	to eat	rice	and	cassava	now	Complete sentence
3a	menapa	pandjenengan	badé	dahar	sekul	kalijan	kaspé	samenika	*Menapa pandjenengan badé dahar sekul kalijan kaspé samenika?*
3		sampéjan		neda					*Menapa sampéjan badé neda sekul kalijan kaspé samenika?*

Level	are	you	going	to eat	rice	and	cassava	now	Complete sentence
1b	apa	pandjenengan	arep	dahar	sega	lan	kaspé	saiki	*Apa pandjenengan arep dahar sega lan kaspé saiki?*
1a		kowé		neda					*Apa sampéjan arep neda sega lan kaspé saiki?*
1		sampéjan		mangan					*Apa kowé arep mangan sega lan kaspé saiki?*

heterogeneity and societal heterogeneity—when both are examined in intragroup perspective—is a major contribution of sociolinguistics to the study of social organization and social change (see Table 5).

4.1 THE SIGNIFICANCE OF PERVASIVE LINGUISTIC DISCONTINUITY

Prior to the development of sociolinguistics, area dialectology had already clearly indicated that discontinuous populations (i.e., populations that lived at some distance from each other or that were impeded in their communication with each other by physical or political barriers) frequently revealed substantial phonological and morphological differences between their language systems. Where such differences did not obtain despite the absence of communicational frequency and sociocultural unity, recency of settlement from a single source or other similar unifying factors (conquest, religious conversion, etc.) were assumed and encountered. Indeed, if we view the entire world as a single geographic area, we tend to find similar (i.e., genetically related) languages clustered contiguously or closely to each other ("language families" are normally clustered geographically, except for the confounding fact of colonization and distant migration). Some parts of the world, of course, are famous for their concentration of highly diversified languages found in close proximity to each other. However, these same areas are also noted for their mountains, jungles, deserts, and rivers, i.e., for barriers that have limited travel, commerce, and common endeavor.

More difficult to explain are those variations in language and behavior that are *coterritorial*. In such instances sheer physical distance cannot be invoked as either a causal or a maintenance variable for the variations encountered. In such cases cultural and social factors alone must be examined and they alone must be meaningfully related to the *degree* and *kind* of language differences noted. In reviewing coterritorial linguistic diversity throughout history it becomes clear that it can be maintained in an extremely stable manner. Throughout the world—but particularly throughout the ancient and traditional world—populations have lived side by side for centuries without learning each other's languages and without significantly modifying or giving up their distinctly discontinuous repertoires. Except for the relatively few middlemen that connect them (merchants, translators, etc.), such populations represent distinct speech communities although they may be citizens of the same country, of the same city, and, indeed, of the same neighborhood. However, the maintenance of such well-nigh complete linguistic and sociocultural cleavage—equal in degree and kind to that encountered between territorially discontinuous populations—is often indicative of population relocation sometime in the past that has subsequently been buttressed and maintained by sociocultural (including ethnic and religious) differences. The *former* differences are responsible for the origin of the differences noted by Blanc (1964) between the Moslem Arabic, Christian Arabic, and Jewish Arabic of Baghdad. The *latter* differences are responsible for the *maintenance* of these cleavages in as sharp a manner, or nearly so, as initially established.

While it may often be relatively difficult to overcome the cleavage between separate but coterritorial speech communities, it is not impossible to do so. The forced conversion of various Jewish and Christian communities during certain periods of Islamic rule, the urban-industrial assimilation of hitherto rural or small-town immigrants and their children in the United States (Nahirny and Fishman 1965, Fishman 1965a, 1965e, 1966c), the very similar assimilation of tribal populations moving to Wolof-speaking Dakar (Tabouret-Keller 1968), the Hellenization and Romanization of many "barbarian" elites in ancient Rome and Alexandria, the convergence between illiterate speakers of Marati and Kannada in India (Gumperz 1967)—these are all examples of the fusing into one of populations that originally functioned as largely separate though coterritorial speech communities. Conversely, the mutual alienation of populations that originally considered themselves to be united can create fargoing linguistic differences between them where none, or few, existed previously. In general, the more fargoing the linguistic differences between any two coterritorial populations (i.e., the more the differences are basically grammatical—syntactic and morphological—rather than primarily phonological or lexical), the more their linguistic repertoires are compartmentalized from each other so as to reveal little if any interference, and the more they reveal functionally different verbal repertoires in terms of the sociolinguistic units reviewed in Section 4, above—then the greater the interactional and sociocultural gap between the speech communities involved.

4.2 MORE MARGINAL SYSTEMATIC DISCONTINUITY

However, most coterritorial populations that differ in verbal repertoire cannot be considered fully separate speech communities, even if the differences between them can be considered as basically geographic in origin. There are very many areas today, primarily urban in nature, where subpopulations that differ in social class, religion, or ethnic affiliation nevertheless view themselves as sharing many common norms and standards and where these subpopulations interact sufficiently (or are sufficiently exposed to common educational institutions and media) to be termed a single speech community. It is hardly surprising, therefore, that the linguistic differences between such sociocultural subpopulations (or networks) within the same speech community are linguistically marginal (i.e., lexical and, to a lesser degree, morphological and phonological) rather than syntactic and all-embracing. It is clear that the social-class variation that exists in New York City English is of this kind rather than of the kind that develops between clearly separate, noninteracting, and mutually alienated speech communities. One of the surest indications of this is the fact that (if we delete features attributable to Southern Negro, Puerto Rican, and other recent geographically derived differences) few of the characteristic phonological features of lower-class speech in New York are entirely absent from the speech of other classes in New York City, just as few of the characteristic phonological features of its upper-class speech are entirely lacking from the lower-class speech of that city. What does differentiate between the social classes in New York is the degree to which certain phonological *variables* are realized in *certain ways* on *particular occasions* rather than their complete absence from the repertoire of any particular class.

Labov's recent studies of the phonological correlates of social stratification (1964, 1965, 1966a, 1966b, 1968) illustrate this point. In one of his studies (1964) Labov gathered four different samples of speech (each by a different method calculated to elicit material approximating a different kind of speech situation) from four different social classes of informants. Studying such variables as *th* (as in thing, through), *eh* the height of the vowel in bad, ask, half, dance, *r* (the presence or absence of final and preconsonantal /r/) and *oh* (the height of the vowel in off, chocolate, all, coffee) Labov found that *all* social classes yielded some values of each variable in nearly every speech situation (see Figure 3). However, the differences between the social classes remained clear enough. Lower-class speakers were less likely to pronounce the fricative form of the [æ] than were working-class speakers; working-class speakers, less likely to pronounce it than lower-middle-class speakers; lower-middle-class speakers, less likely to yield it than upper-middle-class speakers. Speakers of all classes were more likely to pronounce the standard fricative form (rather than the substandard affricate [t] or lenis stop [t]) in reading word lists than they were when reading passages; more likely to pronounce it when reading passages than when being interviewed (= careful speech); more likely to pronounce it when being interviewed

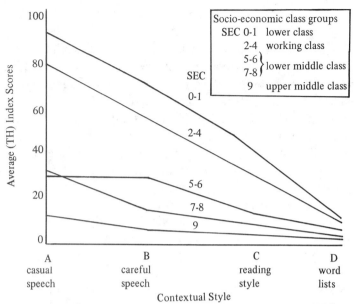

FIGURE 3A. Class Stratification Diagram for (th). (Labov 1964)

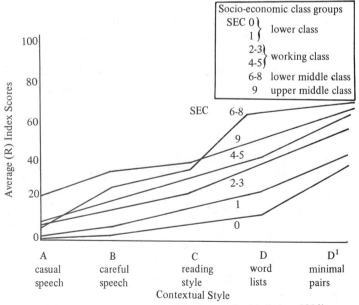

FIGURE 3B. Class Stratification Diagram for (r). (Labov 1964)

than when recounting "a situation where you thought you were in serious danger of being killed" (= casual speech).

This may be considered a hallmark of social-class differences in speech where the classes as a whole are still members of the same speech community. As long as individuals in each class can differ in repertoire, depending on their personal opportunities and experiences with respect to interaction with various speech networks, there can be no complete discontinuity in repertoires, no complete freezing of social-class position, and no overriding alienation into separate religious, ethnic, or other relatively fixed and immutable speech communities.

Of course, not all variables yield such dramatic and clearcut social class differences as those found in connection with *th* in New York. With respect to *r, eh,* and *oh* Labov's data reveal much more *similarity* between the several social classes, although the differences between contexts and between classes remain quite clear. Labov's data also reveal a recurring *reversal* with respect to the lower-middle-class performance on word and passage reading lists. This reversal, dubbed *hypercorrection,* shows the lower middle class to be more "correct" (more careful, more inclined to utilize the standard or cultured pronunciation) than is the upper middle class at its most correct or careful. Such a reversal may well indicate a variable that has become a stereotype rather than merely a marker of class position. As such it tends to be used (or overused) by those who are insecure about their social position, i.e., by those who are striving to create a more advantageous social position for themselves in a speech community in which upward social mobility seems to be possible. This explanation is not dissimilar from that which Labov utilized to explain observed differences in centralization of /ai/ and /au/ in Martha's Vineyard (1963). Such centralization was most common among minority-group members (of Portuguese and Indian extraction) who sought to *stress their positive orientation to Martha's Vineyard,* rather than among the old Yankees, whose feelings toward the Vineyard were more low-keyed and required no linguistic underscoring. Whether consciously employed or not the "Pygmalian effect" in language is a striking indicator of reference group behavior and of social aspirations more generally (Ross 1956).

4.3 NONPROLETARIANS OF ALL REGIONS, UNITE!

In a relatively open and fluid society there will be few characteristics of lower-class speech that are not also present (albeit to a lesser extent) in the speech of the working and lower middle classes. Whether we look to phonological features such as those examined by Labov or to morphological units such as those reported by Fischer (1958) (Fischer studied the variation between -in' and -ing for the present participle ending, i.e., runnin' vs. running—and found that the former realization was more common when children were talking to each other than when they were talking to him, more common among boys than among girls, and more common among "typical boys" than among "model boys"), we find not a clear-cut cleavage between the social classes but a difference in rate of realization of particular variants of particular variables for particular contexts. Even the widely publicized distinction between the "restricted code" of lower-class speakers and the "elaborated code" of middle-class speakers (Bernstein 1964, 1966) is of this type, since Bernstein includes the cocktail party and the religious service among the social situations in which restricted codes are realized. Thus, even in the somewhat more stratified British setting the middle class is found to share some of the features of what is considered to be "typically" lower-class speech. Obviously then, "typicality," if it has any meaning at all in relatively open societies, must refer largely to repertoire *range* rather than to unique features of the repertoire.

Those speech networks with the widest range of experiences, interactions, and interests are also those that have the greatest linguistic repertoire range. In many speech communities these networks are likely to be in one or another of the middle classes, since some networks within these classes are most likely to maintain direct contact with the lower and working classes below them (in employer-employee, teacher-pupil, and other role relationships), as well as with the upper class above them (in educational, recreational, and cultural interactions). However, whereas the repertoire ranges of the upper and lower classes are likely to be equally discontinuous (even if restricted), there is likely to be a very major distinction between them if the larger speech community (the region, the country) is considered. Lower classes tend to be regionally and occupationally separated from each other to a far greater extent than do upper and middle classes (Gumperz 1958). Thus there may well be several different lower-class varieties in a country (depending on regional and on occupational or other specializations), while at the same time upper and upper-middle-class speech may attain greater uniformity and greater regional neutrality. The more advantaged classes travel more frequently, engage in joint enterprises more frequently, control the agencies of language uniformation (schools, media, language-planning agencies, and government per se). They more quickly arrive at a common standard, at least for formal occasions, than do the lower classes, who remain fragmented and parochial. Differences such as these are illustrated in Nancy Tanner's case study of an Indonesian elite group (1967). Whereas the lower classes speak only their local ethnic language, the middle and upper classes also speak several varieties of Indonesian (including a regionally neutral variety that is least influenced by local characteristics), and the elites speak English and Dutch as well. One can predict that as these elites lose their local ties and affiliations and assume Pan-Indonesian roles, establishing speech communities of their own in Djakarta and in a few other large cities, their need for local languages and for locally influenced and informal Indonesian will lessen and their stylistic variation will proceed, as it has with elites in England, France,

Germany, Russia, and elsewhere in the world, via contrasts with foreign tongues (see Figure 4).

4.4 DIVERSIFICATION VS. MASSIFICATION

One further consideration deserves at least brief attention in our review of societal differentiation and language variation; namely, the common view that there is a trend toward over-all uniformation, in lanugage and in other social behavior, as industrialization progresses (Bell 1961; Boulding 1963; Hertzler 1965; Hodges 1964). It is undeniable that life in urbanized and industrial countries is in some ways more uni-form than it is in countries where local and regional partic-ularisms remain relatively untouched. Nevertheless, it seems to be erroneous to think of preindustrial rural heterogeneity and industrial urban homogeneity as either accurate or mutually exclusive designations. Both stages of development seem to foster as well as to inhibit certain kinds of uniforma-

FIGURE 4. Functional Specialization of Codes in Indonesia and Among the Case Study Group

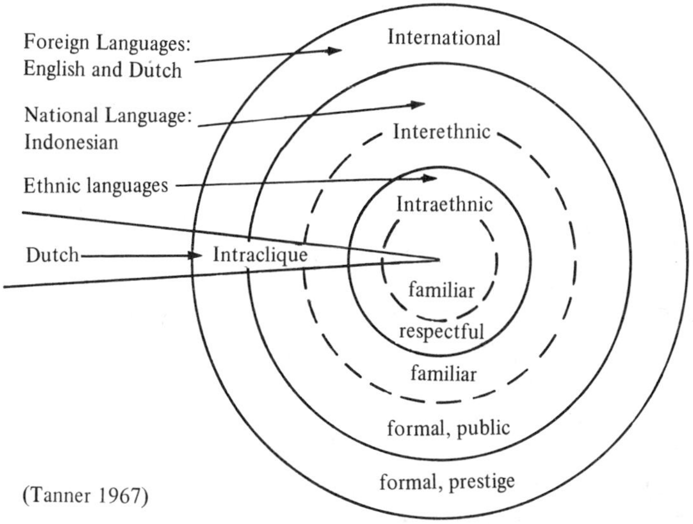

Foreign Languages:
English and Dutch

National Language:
Indonesian

Ethnic languages

Dutch

International

Interethnic

Intraethnic

Intraclique

familiar

respectful

familiar

formal, public

formal, prestige

(Tanner 1967)

tion and differentiation, in language as well as in other aspects of behavior.

Certainly, the preindustrial rural society is not so internally heterogeneous as is the urban society with its variety of classes, religions, ethnic groups, and interest groups. Thus, the supposedly uniformizing effect of urbanization and industrialization must pertain to interregional or interurban comparisons rather than to intraurban or intralocal ones. Nevertheless, the best available evidence indicates that no trend toward interregional homogeneity in religion, politics, or other generalized behaviors is apparent in the United States (Glenn 1966, 1967a, 1967b), nor are such trends apparent in other countries, such as England, France, Holland, or Belgium, that have been industrialized or urbanized for the greatest length of time. There the differences in values, tastes, and social and political orientations between manual and nonmanual workers seem to be as great or greater than they are today in the United States (Hamilton 1965; Bonjean 1966; Schnore 1966; Broom and Glenn 1966, etc.).

At the language level both uniformation and differentiation are found to go on simultaneously, indicative of the fact that the traditional and the modern are frequently *combined* into new constellations rather than *displaced* one by the other. Uniformation pressures seem to be strongest in conjunction with only certain varieties within a speech community's verbal repertoire as well as in conjunction with only some of the interaction networks of that community. The language variety associated with school, government, and industry tends to be adopted differentially, the degree of its adoption varying with the degree of interaction in these domains. Not only need such adoption not be displacive (particularly when populations remain in their former places of residence), but—even though the adoption may be quite uniform and official for an entire country—it may remain an entirely passive rather than an active component in the repertoire of many interaction networks. Thus, even though television viewing and radio listening are most frequent and prolonged among the lower classes, their overt repertoires seem to be little influenced by such viewing or listening.

Finally, it should be recognized that urbanization may also foster certain kinds of differentiation. Whereas the number of different ethnic groups (and, therefore, the number of mutually exclusive language groups) may decline, new social differentiations and new occupational and interest groups normally follow in the wake of industrialization. These latter commonly develop sociolects and specialized usages of their own, thus expanding the repertoires of many speakers. Even the rise of languages of wider communication frequently results in differentiation rather than in uniformation. The spread of English as a second language in the past fifty years has resulted in there being more varieties of English today (including Indian English, East African English, Franglais, Spanglish, and others) rather than less. It is, of course, true that certain languages, now as in the past, are in danger of dying out. Nevertheless, others, frequently regarded as "mere varieties" rather than as full-fledged languages, are constantly being "born" in terms of differentiating themselves within the linguistic repertoires of certain interaction networks and, at times, of entire speech communities. Modernization is a complex phenomenon. While it depresses the status and decreases the number of speakers of certain varieties (e.g., in recent years: Frisian, Romansch, Landsmal, Yiddish), it raises the status and increases the speakers of others (Macedonian, Neo-Melanesian, Indonesian, Swahili, etc.).

Our own American environment is an atypical example. It reveals the uniformation that results from the rapid urbanization and industrialization of *dislocated* populations. We must not confuse the American experience with that of the rest of the world (Greenberg 1965). In addition we must come to recognize that American uniformation, whether in speech or in diet, is a surface phenomenon. It is an added variety to the repertoires that are still there and that are still substantial if we but scratch a little deeper (Fishman 1967).

Section V

SOCIETAL BILINGUALISM: STABLE AND TRANSITIONAL

Societal bilingualism has been referred to so many times in the previous pages that it is time that we paused to consider it in its own right rather than as a means of illustrating more general sociolinguistic phenomena. The psychological literature on bilingualism is so much more extensive than its sociological counterpart that workers in the former field have often failed to establish contact with those in the latter. It is the purpose of this section to relate these two research traditions to each other by tracing the interaction between their two major constructs: bilingualism (on the part of psychologists and psycholinguists) and diglossia (on the part of sociologists and sociolinguists).

5.1 DIGLOSSIA

In the few years that have elapsed since Ferguson (1959a) first advanced it, the term diglossia has not only become widely accepted by sociolinguists and sociologists of language, but it has been further extended and refined. Initially it was used in connection with a *society* that recognized two (or more) languages for introsocietal communication. The use within a single society of several separate codes (and their stable maintenance rather than the displacement of one by the other over time) was found to be dependent on each code's serving functions distinct from those considered appropriate for the other code. Whereas one set of behaviors, attitudes, and values supported, and was expressed in, one language, another set of behaviors attitudes, and values supported and was expressed in the other. Both sets of behaviors, attitudes, and values were fully accepted as culturally legitimate and complementary (i.e., nonconflictual) and indeed, little if any conflict between them was possible in view of the functional separation between them. This separation was most often along the lines of an H(igh) language, on the one hand, utilized in conjunction with religion, education, and other aspects of high culture, and an L(ow) language, on the other hand, utilized in conjunction with everyday pursuits of hearth, home, and lower work sphere. Ferguson spoke of H as "superposed" because it is normally learned later and in a more formal setting than L and is thereby superimposed on it.

To this original edifice others have added several significant considerations. Gumperz (1961, 1962, 1964a, 1964b, 1966) is primarily responsible for our greater awareness that diglossia exists not only in multilingual societies which officially recognize several "languages," and not only in societies that utilize vernacular and classical varieties, but also in societies which employ separate dialects, registers, or *functionally differentiated language varieties of whatever kind.* He has also done the lion's share of the work in providing the conceptual apparatus by means of which investigators of multilingual speech communities seek to discern the societal patterns that govern the use of one variety rather than another, particularly at the level of small group interaction. Fishman (1964, 1965a, 1965c, 1965d, 1965e, 1966a, 1968c), on the other hand, has attempted to trace the maintenance of diglossia as well as its disruption at the national or societal level. In addition he has attempted to relate diglossia to psychologically pertinent considerations such as compound and coordinate bilingualism (1965b). The present section represents an extension and integration of these several previous attempts.

For purposes of simplicity it seems best to represent the possible relationships between bilingualism and diglossia by means of a fourfold table such as that shown in Figure 5.

5.2 SPEECH COMMUNITIES CHARACTERIZED BY BOTH DIGLOSSIA AND BILINGUALISM

The first quadrant of Figure 5 refers to those speech communities in which both diglossia and bilingualism are widespread. At times such communities comprise an entire nation, but of course this requires extremely widespread (if not all-pervasive) bilingualism, and as a result there are really few nations that are fully bilingual and diglossic. An approximation to such a nation is Paraguay, where more than half of the population speaks both Spanish and Guaraní (Rubin 1962, 1968). A substantial proportion of the formerly monolingual rural population has added Spanish to its linguistic repertoire in connection with matters of education, religion, government, and high culture (although in the rural areas social distance or status stressing more generally may still be expressed in Guaraní). On the other hand, the vast majority of city dwellers (being relatively new from the country)

FIGURE 5. The Relationships Between Bilingualism and Diglossia

BILINGUALISM	*DIGLOSSIA*	
	+	−
+	1. Both diglossia and bilingualism	2. Bilingualism without diglossia
−	3. Diglossia without bilingualism	4. Neither diglossia nor bilingualism

maintain Guaraní for matters of intimacy and primary group solidarity, even in the midst of their more newly acquired Spanish urbanity (see Figure 6). Note that Guaraní is not an "official" language (i.e., recognized and utilized for purposes of government, formal education, the courts, etc.) in Paraguay, although it was finally recognized as a "national language" at the 1967 constitutional convention. It is not uncommon for the H variety alone to be recognized as "official" in diglossic settings without this fact threatening

FIGURE 6. National Bilingualism in Paraguay: Ordered Dimensions in the Choice of Language in a Diglossic Society.

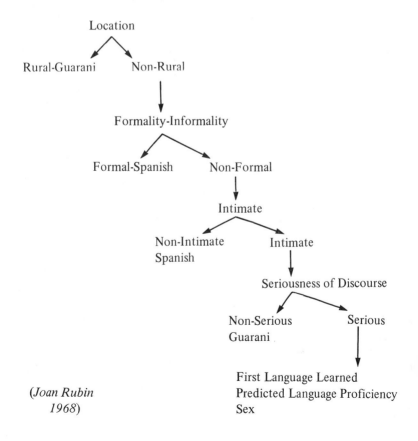

the acceptance or the stability of the L variety within the speech community. However, the existence of a single "official" language should not divert the investigator from recognizing the fact of widespread and stable multilingualism at the levels of societal and interpersonal functioning (see Table 6).

Below the level of nationwide functioning there are many more examples of stable diglossia co-occurring with widespread bilingualism. The Swiss-German cantons may be mentioned, since their entire population of school age and older alternates between High German (H) and Swiss German (L) each with its own firmly established and highly valued functions (Ferguson 1959a; Weinreich, U. 1951, 1953). Traditional (pre-World War I) Eastern European Jewish males communicated in Hebrew (H) and Yiddish (L). In more recent days many of their descendents have continued to do so in various countries of resettlement, even while adding to their repertoire a Western language (notably English) in certain domains of *intragroup* communication as well as for broader *intergroup* contacts (Fishman 1965a, 1965e; Weinreich, U. 1953; Weinreich, M. 1953). This development differs signifi-

TABLE 6. Linguistic Unity and Diversity, by World Region.

REGION	\multicolumn{10}{c}{No. of Countries by Percent of Population Speaking Main Language}
	90-100	80-89	70-79	60-69	50-59	40-49	30-39	20-29	10-19	Total 10-100%
Europe	17	4	2	2	2	–	–	–	–	27
East and South Asia	5	3	4	3	1	4	–	1	–	21
Oceania*	2	–	–	–	–	–	–	–	–	2
Middle East and Northern Africa	8	6	2	3	1	2	–	–	–	22
Tropical and Southern Africa	3	–	–	2	5	8	7	5	3	33
The Americas	15	6	–	–	2	2	1	–	–	26
World Total	50	19	8	10	11	16	8	6	3	131

Source: Table 1 (Rustow, D. 1967).
*Not including New Guinea, for which no breakdown by individual languages was available.

cantly from the traditional Eastern European Jewish pattern in which males whose occupational activities brought them into regular contact with various strata of the non-Jewish coterritorial population utilized one or more coterritorial languages (which involved H and L varieties of their own, such as Russian, German, or Polish on the one hand, and Ukrainian, Byelorussian, or "Baltic" varieties, on the other), but did so for *intergroup* purposes almost exclusively. A similar example is that of upper and upper-middle-class males throughout the Arabic world who use classical (Koranic) Arabic for traditional Islamic studies, vernacular (Egyptian, Syrian, Lebanese, Iraqi, etc.) Arabic for informal conversation, and, not infrequently, also a Western language (French or English, most usually) for purposes of *intragroup* scientific or technological communication (Blanc 1964; Ferguson 1959a; Nader 1962).

All of the foregoing examples have in common the existence of a fairly large and complex speech community, so that its members have available to them both a range of *compartmentalized* roles as well as ready *access* to these roles. If the *role repertoires* of these speech communities were of lesser range, then their *linguistic repertoires* would also be-(come) more restricted in range, with the result that one or more separate languages or varieties would be(come) superflous. In addition, were the roles not compartmentalized, i.e., were they not *kept separate* by dint of association with quite separate (though complementary) values, domains of activity, and everyday situations, one language (or variety) would displace the other as role and value distinctions merged and became blurred. Finally, were widespread access not available to the range of compartmentalized roles (and compartmentalized languages or varieties), then the bilingual population would be a small, privileged caste or class (as it is or was throughout most of traditional India or China) rather than a broadly based population segment.

These observations must lead us to the conclusion that many modern speech communities that are normally thought of as monolingual are, rather, marked by both diglossia and bilingualism, if their several registers are viewed as separate varieties or languages in the same sense as the examples listed above. Wherever speech communities exist whose speakers engage in a considerable range of roles (and this is coming to be the case for all but the extremely upper and lower levels of complex societies), wherever access to several roles is encouraged or facilitated by powerful social institutions and processes, and finally, wherever the roles are clearly differentiated (in terms of when, where, and with whom they are felt to be appropriate), both diglossia and bilingualism may be said to exist. The benefit of this approach to the topic at hand is that it provides a single theoretical framework for viewing bilingual speech communities and speech communities whose linguistic diversity is realized through varieties not (yet) recognized as constituting separate "languages." Thus, rather than becoming fewer in modern times, the number of speech communities characterized by diglossia and the widespread command of diversified linguistic repertoires has increased greatly as a consequence of modernization and growing social complexity (Fishman 1966b). In such communities each generation begins anew on a monolingual or restricted repertoire base of hearth and home and must be rendered bilingual or provided with a fuller repertoire by the formal institutions of education, religion, government, or the work sphere. In diglossic-bilingual speech communities children do *not* attain their full repertoires at home or in their neighborhood play groups. Indeed, those who most commonly remain at home or in the home neighborhood (the preschool young and the postwork old) are most likely to be functionally monolingual, as Lieberson's tables on French-English bilingualism in Montreal amply reveal (see Table 7).

TABLE 7. Percentage Bilingual, by Age and Sex, Montreal Area, 1931-61.

Age	MALES					FEMALES				
	Montreal-Verdun		Montreal-Outremont-Verdun			Montreal-Verdun		Montreal-Outremont-Verdun		
	1931 (1)	1941 (2)	1941 (3)	1951 (4)	1961 (5)	1931 (6)	1941 (7)	1941 (8)	1951 (9)	1961 (10)
0- 4	4.1	5.7	5.7	3.3	2.5	4.0	5.6	5.7	3.4	2.5
5- 9	18.2	11.3	11.5	9.7	9.9	18.0	11.5	11.8	9.7	9.6
10-14	43.4	22.2	22.6	20.5	22.4	41.4	21.9	22.3	20.1	21.9
15-19	62.4	51.4	51.7	50.6	49.6	54.7	43.1	43.5	44.5	46.7
20-24	67.2	67.1	67.2	64.9	59.4	53.3	51.5	51.7	48.2	44.4
25-34	61.9	68.8	68.8	68.8	59.7	49.0	47.8	48.1	47.8	41.1
35-44	62.2	63.6	63.7	68.1	65.3	44.5	40.9	41.2	45.2	45.5
45-54	59.3	60.3	60.3	62.7	63.6	41.6	35.6	36.0	37.4	42.6
55-64	57.4	53.7	53.8	57.3	57.2	37.1	31.2	31.6	30.8	34.5
65-69	56.4	49.4	49.6	49.7	52.0	34.3	28.0	28.5	26.5	28.5
70+	51.2	42.9	43.3	42.2	44.0	31.2	24.4	24.7	23.5	24.5

(Lieberson 1965).

5.3 DIGLOSSIA WITHOUT BILINGUALISM

Departing from the co-occurrence of bilingualism and diglossia we come first to polities in which diglossia obtains, whereas bilingualism is generally absent (quadrant 3). Here we find two or more speech communities united politically, religiously, and/or economically into a single functioning unit notwithstanding the sociocultural cleavages that separate them. At the level of this larger (but not always voluntary) unity, two or more languages or varieties must be recognized as obtaining. However one (or both) of the speech communities involved is (are) marked by such relatively impermeable group boundaries that for "outsiders" (and this may well mean all those not born into the speech community, i.e., an emphasis on ascribed rather than on achieved status) role access and linguistic access are severely restricted. At the same time linguistic repertoires in one or both groups are limited due to role specialization.

Examples of such situations are not hard to find (see, e.g., the many instances listed by Kloss 1966). Pre-World War I European elites often stood in this relationship with their countrymen, the elites speaking French or some other fashionable H tongue for their *intragroup* purposes (at various times and in various places: Danish, Salish, Provencal, Russian, etc.) and the masses speaking another, not necessarily linguistically related, language for their intragroup purposes. Since the majority of elites and the majority of the masses never interacted with one another they *did not form a single speech community* (i.e., their linguistic repertoires were discontinuous) and their intercommunications were via translators or interpreters (a certain sign of *intragroup* monolingualism). Since the majority of the elites and the majority of the masses led lives characterized by extremely narrow role repertoires, their linguistic repertoires also were too narrow to permit widespread societal bilingualism to develop. Nevertheless, the body politic in all of its economic and national manifestations tied these two groups together into a "unity" that revealed an upper and a lower class, each with a language appropriate to its own restricted concerns. Some have suggested that the modicum of direct interaction that does occur between servants and masters who differ in mother tongue brings into being the marginal languages (pidgins) for which such settings are known.

Thus, the existence of national diglossia does *not* imply widespread bilingualism among rural or recently urbanized African groups (as distinguished from somewhat more Westernized populations in those settings); or among most lower-caste Hindus, as distinguished from their more fortunate compatriots the Brahmins, or among most lower-class French Canadians, as distinguished from their upper and upper-middle-class city cousins, etc. In general, this pattern is characteristic of polities that are economically underdeveloped and unmobilized, combining groups that are locked into opposite extremes of the social spectrum and, therefore, groups that operate within extremely restricted and discontinuous linguistic repertoires (Friederich 1962). Obviously, such polities are bound to experience language problems as their social patterns alter in the direction of industrialization, widespread literacy and education, democratization, and modernization more generally. Since few polities that exhibit diglossia without bilingualism developed out of prior sociocultural consensus or unity, any educational, political, or economic development experienced by their lower classes is likely to lead to secessionism or to demands for equality for their submerged languages. The linguistic states of Eastern Europe and India, and the language problems of Wales, Canada, and Belgium stem from origins such as these. This is the pattern of development that may yet convulse modern West African nations if their de-ethnicized Westernized elites continue to fail to foster widespread and stable bilingual speech communities that incorporate the masses and that recognize both the official language of wider communication and the local languages of hearth and home.

5.4 BILINGUALISM WITHOUT DIGLOSSIA

We turn next to those situations in which bilingualism obtains, whereas diglossia is generally absent (quadrant 2). Here we see even more clearly than before that bilingualism is essentially a characterization of *individual* linguistic versatility whereas *diglossia is a characterization of the societal allocation of functions* to different languages or varieties. Under what circumstances do bilinguals function without the benefit of a well-understood and widely accepted social consensus as to which language is to be used between *which* interlocutors, for communication concerning *what* topics or for *what* purposes? Under what circumstances do the varieties or languages involved lack well-defined or protected separate functions? Briefly put, these are circumstances of rapid social change, of great social unrest, of widespread abandonment of prior norms before the consolidation of new ones. Children typically become bilingual at a very early age, when they are still largely confined to home and neighborhood, since their elders (both adults and school aged) carry into the domains of intimacy a language learned outside its confines. Formal institutions tend to render individuals increasingly monolingual in a language other than that of hearth and home. Ultimately, the language of school and government replaces the language of home and neighborhood precisely because it provides status in the later domains as well (see Tables 8 and 9).

Many studies of bilingualism and intelligence or of bilingualism and school achievement have been conducted within the context of bilingualism without diglossia (for a review see Macnamara 1966), often without sufficient understanding on the part of investigators that this was but one of several possible contexts for the study of bilingualism. As a result, many of the purported "disadvantages" of bilingualism have been falsely generalized to the phenomenon at large rather than related to the absence or presence of social patterns which reach substantially beyond bilingualism (Fishman 1965b; 1966a).

TABLE 8. Frequency of Mother Tongue Use in Conversations by Oldest and Youngest Children of Four Ethnic Backgrounds.* (Fishman 1966c)

In Conversation with:	German			Jewish			Polish			Ukrainian		
	Almost Always N %	Frequently N %	Almost Never N %	Almost Always N %	Frequently N %	Almost Never N %	Almost Always N %	Frequently N %	Almost Never N %	Almost Always N %	Frequently N %	Almost Never N %
Grandparents	6 26.1	6 26.1	11 47.8	6 20.0	9 30.0	15 50.0	15 57.6	5 19.2	6 23.2	26 96.3	—	1 3.7
Father	7 18.4	10 26.4	21 55.2	5 15.0	23 34.3	34 50.7	22 38.3	17 26.7	21 35.0	42 84.0	6 12.0	2 4.0
Mother	5 16.1	4 12.9	22 71.0	5 9.8	19 37.4	27 52.9	16 29.1	14 25.4	25 45.5	41 89.1	5 10.9	—
Brothers and Sisters	2 8.7	2 8.7	19 82.6	—	7 18.9	30 81.1	7 19.4	5 13.8	24 66.7	20 50.0	18 45.0	2 5.0
Friends	3 10.0	7 23.3	20 66.7	—	10 22.7	34 77.3	4 9.8	9 21.9	28 68.3	15 27.3	20 36.4	20 36.4
Husband and Wife	2 11.1	1 5.6	15 83.3	—	1 4.5	21 95.5	3 15.0	—	17 85.0	4 36.4	3 27.3	4 36.4
Own Child	1 5.6	3 16.7	14 77.8	—	1 5.3	18 94.7	3 20.0	—	12 80.0	4 50.0	3 37.5	1 12.5

*Data reported by parents. The German and Polish parents studied were primarily second-generation individuals. The Jewish and Ukranian parents studied were primarily first-generation individuals. All parents were ethnic cultural or organizational "leaders."

TABLE 9. 1940-1960 Totals for 23 Non-English Mother Tongues in the USA (Fishman 1966c).

Language	1940 Total	1960 Total	Total Change	
			n	%
Norwegian	658,220	321,774	−336,446	−51.1%
Swedish	830,900	415,597	−415,303	−50.0%
Danish	226,740	147,619	− 79,121	−65.1%
Dutch/Flemish	289,580	321,613	+ 32,033	+11.1%
French	1,412,060	1,043,220	−368,840	−26.1%
German	4,949,780	3,145,772	−1,804,008	−36.4%
Polish	2,416,320	2,184,936	−231,384	−9.6%
Czech	520,440	217,771	−302,669	−58.2%
Slovak	484,360	260,000	−224,360	−46.3%
Hungarian	453,000	404,114	−48,886	−10.8%
Serbo-Croatian	153,080	184,094	+31,014	+20.3%
Slovenian	178,640	67,108	−111,532	−62.4%
Russian	585,080	460,834	−124,246	−21.2%
Ukrainian	83,600	252,974	+169,374	+202.6%
Lithuanian	272,680	206,043	−66,637	−24.4%
Finnish	230,420	110,168	−120,252	−52.2%
Rumanian	65,520	58,019	−7,501	−11.4%
Yiddish	1,751,100	964,605	−786,495	−44.9%
Greek	273,520	292,031	+18,511	+6.8%
Italian	3,766,820	3,673,141	−93,679	−2.5%
Spanish	1,861,400	3,335,961	+1,474,561	+79.2%
Portuguese	215,660	181,109	−34,551	−16.0%
Arabic	107,420	103,908	−3,512	−3.3%
Total	21,786,540	18,352,351	−3,434,189	−15.8%

In 1940 the numerically strongest mother tongues in the United States were German, Italian, Polish, Spanish, Yiddish, and French, in that order. Each of these languages was claimed by approximately a million and a half or more individuals. In 1960 these same languages remained the "big six" although their order had changed to Italian, Spanish, German, Polish, French, and Yiddish. Among them, only Spanish registered gains (and substantial gains at that) in this 20-year interval. The losses among the "big six" varied from a low of 2.5% for Italian to a high of 44.9% for Yiddish. The only other languages to gain in overall number of claimants during this period (disregarding the generational distribution of such gains) were Ukrainian, Serbo-Croatian, "Dutch"/ Flemish, and Greek. The greatest gain of all was that of Ukrainian

(202.6%!). Most mother tongues, including five of the "big six", suffered substantial losses during this period, the sharpest being that of Danish (65.1%). All in all, the 23 non-English mother tongues for which a 1940-1960 comparison is possible lost approximately one-sixth of their claimants during this interval. Yet the total number of claimants of non-English mother tongues in the United States is still quite substantial, encompassing nearly 11% of the total 1960 population (and an appreciably higher proportion of the white population).[6]

---

[6] The 1940 and 1960 totals shown in Table 9 must not be taken as the totals for *all* non-English mother tongue claimants in those years. Figures for Armenian were reported in 1940 but not in 1960. Figures for Chinese and Japanese were reported in 1960 but not in 1940. Total figures for "All other" languages were reported in both years. None of these inconsistent or non-specific listings are included in Table 2.4. Adding in these figures as well as the necessary generational estimates based upon them, the two totals would become 1940: 22,036,240; 1960: 19,381,786.

The history of industrialization in the Western world (as well as in those parts of Africa and Asia which have experienced industrialization under Western "auspices") is such that the means (capital, plant, organization) of production have often been controlled by one speech community while the productive manpower was drawn from another (Deutsch 1966). Initially, both speech communities may have maintained their separate diglossia-with-bilingualism patterns or, alternatively, that of an overarching diglossia without bilingualism. In either case, the needs as well as the consequences of rapid and massive industrialization and urbanization were frequently such that members of the speech community providing productive manpower rapidly abandoned their traditional sociocultural patterns and learned (or were taught) the language associated with the means of production much earlier than their absorption into the sociocultural patterns and privileges to which that language pertained. In response to this imbalance some reacted by further stressing the advantages of the newly gained language of education and industry while others reacted by seeking to replace the latter by an elaborated version of their own largely preindustrial, preurban, premobilization tongue.

Under circumstances such as these no well-established, socially recognized and protected functional differentiation of languages obtains in many speech communities of the lower and lower middle classes. Dislocated immigrants and their children (for whom a separate "political solution" is seldom possible) are particularly inclined to use their mother tongue and other tongue for intragroup communication in *seemingly* random fashion (Fishman, Cooper, and Ma 1968; Nahirny and Fishman 1965; Herman 1961). Since the formerly separate roles of the home domain, the school domain, and the work domain are all disturbed by the massive dislocation of values and norms that result from simultaneous immigration and industrialization, the language of work (and of the school) comes to be used at home. As role compartmentalization and value complementarity decrease under the impact of foreign models and massive change, the linguistic repertoire also becomes less compartmentalized. Languages and varieties formerly kept apart come to influence each other phonetically, lexically, semantically, and even grammatically much more than before. Instead of two (or more) carefully separated languages each under the eye of caretaker groups of teachers, preachers, and writers, several intervening varieties may obtain differing in degree of interpenetration. Under these circumstances the languages of immigrants may come to be ridiculed as "debased" and "broken" while at the same time their standard varieties are given no language maintenance support.

Thus, bilingualism without diglossia tends to be transitional both in terms of the linguistic repertoires of speech communities as well as in terms of the speech varieties involved per se. Without separate though complementary norms and values to establish and maintain functional separation of the speech varieties, that language or variety which is fortunate enough to be associated with the predominant drift of social forces tends to displace the other(s). Furthermore, pidginization (the crystallization of new fusion languages or varieties) is likely to set in when members of the "work force" are so dislocated as not to be able to maintain or develop significantly compartmentalized, limited access roles (in which they might be able to safeguard a stable mother-tongue variety), on the one hand, and when social change stops short of permitting them to interact sufficiently with those members of the "power class" who might serve as standard other-tongue models, on the other hand.

5.5 NEITHER DIGLOSSIA NOR BILINGUALISM

Only very small, isolated, and undifferentiated speech communities may be said to reveal neither diglossia nor bilingualism (Gumperz 1962; Fishman 1965c). Given little role differentiation or compartmentalization and frequent face-to-face interaction between all members of the speech community, no fully differentiated registers or varieties may establish themselves. Given self-sufficiency, no regular or significant contacts with other speech communities may be maintained. Nevertheless, such groups—be they bands or clans—are easier to hypothesize than to find (Owens 1965; Sorensen 1967). All speech communities seem to have certain ceremonies or pursuits to which access is limited, if only on an age basis. Thus, all linguistic repertoires contain certain terms that are unknown to certain members of the speech community, and certain terms that are used differently by different subsets of speakers. In addition, metaphorical switching for purposes of emphasis, humor, satire, or criticism must be available in some form even in relatively undifferentiated communities. Finally, such factors as exogamy, warfare, expansion of population, economic growth, and contact with others all lead to internal diversification and, consequently, to repertoire diversification. Such diversification is the beginning of bilingualism. Its societal normification is the hallmark of diglossia. Quadrant four tends to be self-liquidating.

5.6 CONCLUSIONS

Many efforts are now under way to bring to pass a rapprochement between psychological, linguistic, and sociological work on bilingualism. The student of bilingualism, most particularly the student of bilingualism in the context of social issues and social change, should benefit from an awareness of the various possible relationships between individual bilingualism and societal diglossia illustrated in this section. One of the fruits of such awareness will be that problems of transition and dislocation will not be mistaken for the entire gamut of societal bilingualism.

Section VI

SOCIOCULTURAL ORGANIZATION: LANGUAGE CONSTRAINTS AND LANGUAGE REFLECTIONS

One of the major lines of social and behavioral science interest in language during the past century has been that which has claimed that the radically differing structures of the languages of the world constrain the cognitive functioning of their speakers in different ways. It is only in relatively recent years—and partially as a result of the contributions of psycholinguistics and sociolinguistics—that this view (which we shall refer to as the linguistic relativity view) has come to be replaced by others: (a) that languages primarily reflect rather than create sociocultural regularities in values and orientations, and (b) that languages throughout the world share a far larger number of structural universals than has heretofore been recognized. While we cannot here examine the work related to language universals (Greenberg 1966; Osgood 1960), since it is both highly technical and hardly sociolinguistic in nature, we can pause to consider the linguistic relativity view itself as well as the linguistic reflection view which is increasingly coming to replace it in the interests and in the convictions of social scientists.

6.1 GRAMMATICAL STRUCTURE CONSTRAINS COGNITION

The strongest claim of the adherents of linguistic relativity—whether by Whorf (1940, 1941), Hoijer (1951, 1954), Trager (1959), Kluckhohn (1961), or by others—is that cognitive organization is directly constrained by linguistic structure. Some languages recognize far more tenses than do others (see Figure 7). Sone languages recognize gender of nouns (and, therefore, also require markers of gender in the verb and adjective systems), whereas others do not. Some languages build into the verb system recognition of certainty or uncertainty of past, present, or future action. Other languages build into the verb system a recognition of the size, shape, and color of nouns referred to. There are languages that signify affirmation and negation by different sets of pronouns just as there are languages that utilize different sets of pronouns in order to indicate tense and absence or presence of emphasis. Some languages utilize tone and vowel length in their phonological systems, whereas English and most other modern European languages utilize neither. There are languages that utilize only twelve phonemes while others require more than fifty. A list of such striking structural differences between languages could go on and on—without in any way denying that each language is a perfectly adequate instrument (probably the *most* adequate instrument) for expressing the needs and interests of its speakers. That the societies utilizing these very different languages differ one from the other in many ways is obvious to all. Is it not possible, therefore, that these sociocultural differences—including ways of reasoning, perceiving, learning, distinguishing, remembering, etc.—are directly relatable to the structured differences between the languages themselves? The Whorfian hypothesis claims that this is indeed the case (Fishman 1960).

Intriguing though this claim may be it is necessary to admit that many years of intensive research have not succeeded in demonstrating it to be tenable. Although many

Data of Language Characteristics	Data of (Cognitive) Behavior	
	Language data ("cultural themes")	Nonlinguistic data
Lexical or "semantic" characteristics	Level 1	Level 2
Grammatical characteristics	Level 3	Level 4

FIGURE 7. Schematic Systematization of the Whorfian Hypothesis (Fishman 1960).

Level 1 of the Whorfian ("linguistic relativity") hypothesis predicts that speakers of languages that make certain lexical distinctions are enabled thereby to talk about certain matters (for example, different kinds of snow among speakers of Eskimo and different kinds of horses among speakers of Arabic) that cannot as easily be discussed by speakers of languages that do not make these lexical distinctions. Similarly, Level 3 of the Whorfian hypothesis predicts that speakers of languages that possess particular grammatical features (absence of tense in the verb system, as in Hopi, or whether adjectives normally precede or follow the noun, as in English vs. French) predispose these speakers to certain cultural styles or emphases (timelessness; inductiveness vs. deductiveness). These two levels of the Whorfian hypothesis have often been criticized for their anecdotal nature as well as for their circularity in that they utilized verbal evidence for both their independent (causal) and dependent (consequential) variables. Level 2 of the Whorfian hypothesis predicts that the availability of certain lexical items or distinctions enables the speakers of these languages to remember, perceive, or learn certain nonlinguistic tasks more rapidly or completely than can the speakers of languages that lack these particular lexical items or distinctions. This level of the Whorfian hypothesis has been demonstrated several times—most recently and forcefully in connection with the differing color terminologies of English and Zuni—but it is difficult to argue that the absence of lexical items or distinctions in a particular language is more a *cause* of behavioral differences than a *reflection* of the differing sociocultural concerns or norms of its speakers. As soon as speakers of Zuni become interested in orange (color) they devise a term for it. Language relativity should be more stable and less manipulable than that! Level 4 of the Whorfian hypothesis is the most demanding of all. It predicts that grammatical characteristics of languages facilitate or render more difficult various nonlinguistic behaviors on the part of their speakers. This level has yet to be successfully demonstrated via experimental studies of cognitive behavior.

have tried to do so, no one has successfully predicted and demonstrated a cognitive difference between two populations on the basis of the grammatical or other structural differences between their languages. Speakers of tone languages and of vowel-length languages and of many-voweled languages do *not* seem to hear better than do speakers of languages that lack all of these features. Speakers of languages that code for color, shape, and size in the very verb form itself do not tend to categorize or classify a random set of items much differently than do the speakers of languages whose verbs merely encode tense, person, and number (Carroll and Casagrande, 1958). Whorf's claims (1940) that ". . . the background linguistic system [in other words, the grammar] of each language is not merely a reproducing instrument for voicing ideas, but rather is itself the shaper of ideas, the program and guide for the individual's mental activity, for his analysis of impressions, for his synthesis of his mental stock in trade. Formulation of ideas is not an independent process, strictly rational in the old sense, but it is part of a particular grammar and differs, from slightly to greatly, between grammars" seem to be overstated and no one-to-one correspondence between grammatical structure and either cognitive or sociocultural structure measured independently of language has ever been obtained. Several of the basic principles of sociolinguistic theory may help explain why this is so.

In contrast with the older anthropological-linguistic approach of Whorf, Sapir, Kluckhohn, Korzybski, and others who pursued this problem during the first half of the twentieth century, sociolinguistics is less likely to think of *entire languages* or *entire societies* as categorizable or typable in an over-all way. The very concepts of linguistic repertoire, role repertoire, repertoire range, and repertoire compartmentalization argue against any such neat classification once functional realities are brought into consideration. Any reasonably complex speech community contains various speech networks that vary with respect to the nature and ranges of their speech repertoires. Structural features that may be present in the speech of certain interaction networks may be lacking (or marginally represented) in the speech of others. Structural features that may be present in certain varieties within the verbal repertoire of a particular interaction network may be absent (or marginally represented) in other varieties within that very same repertoire. Mother-tongue speakers of language X may be other-tongue speakers of language Y. These two languages may coexist in a stable diglossic pattern throughout the speech community and yet be as structurally different as any two languages chosen at random.

Certainly, all that has been said above about the difficulty in setting up "whole-language" typologies is equally true when we turn to the question of "whole-society" typologies. Role repertoires vary from one interaction network to the next, and roles themselves vary from one situation to the next within the same role repertoire. Distinctions that are appropriately made in one setting are inappropriate in another, and behaviors that occur within certain interaction networks do not occur in still others within the same culture. The existence of structured biculturism is as real as the existence of structured bilingualism, and both of these phenomena tend to counteract any neat and simple linguistic relativity of the kind that Whorf had in mind.

Nevertheless, there are at least two large areas in which a limited degree of linguistic relativity *may* be said to obtain: (a) the structuring of verbal interaction, and (b) the structuring of lexical components. The first area of concern points to the fact that the role of language (when to speak, to whom to speak, the importance of speaking per se relative to inactive silence or relative to other appropriate action) varies greatly from society to society (Hymes 1966). However, this type of relativity has nothing to do with the *structure* of language per se in which Whorf was so interested. The second area of concern deals with lexical taxonomies and with their consequences in cognition and behavior.   However these border on being linguistic *reflections* of sociocultural structure rather than being clearly and solely linguistic *constraints* that inescapably and interminably must bring about the particular behaviors to which they are supposedly related. It is to a consideration of these lexical taxonomies that we now turn.

6.2 LEXICAL STRUCTURE CONSTRAINS COGNITION

For many years it was believed that the only tightly structured levels of language were the grammatical (morphological and syntactic), on the one hand, and the phonological, on the other. These two levels certainly received the brunt of linguistic attention and constituted the levels of analysis of which linguists were most proud in their interactions with other social and behavioral scientists. By contrast, the lexical level was considered to be unstructured and exposed to infinite expansion (as words were added to any language) and infinite interference (as words were borrowed from other languages). A small but hardy group of lexicographers (dictionary makers) and etymologists (students of word origins) continued to be enamored of words per se, but the majority of linguists acted as though the lexicon were the black sheep, rather than a bona fide member in good standing, of the linguistic family. The discovery of structured parsimony in parts of the lexicon has done much to revive linguistic interest in the lexical level of analysis. The discovery as such is one in which psychologists, anthropologists, and sociologists were at least every bit as active as were linguists themselves. This may also explain why the interrelationship between lexical organization *and* behavioral organization has been so prominent in conjunction with the investigation of lexical structure.

The psychological contributions to this area of analysis take us back to one level of the Whorfian hypothesis (see Level 2 in Figure 7). Psychologists had long before demonstrated that the availability of verbal labels was an asset in learning, perception, and memory tasks (see, e.g., Carmichael et al. 1932; Lehmann 1889; Maier 1930). A new generation of psychologists has recently set out to determine whether this can be demonstrated both interlinguistically (i.e., by comparing different languages) as well as intralinguistically (i.e., within a given language) on a structured set of behaviors that correspond *to a structured portion of lexicon.*

They chose the color spectrum to work with because it is a real continuum that tends to be environmentally present in all cultures. Nevertheless, the investigators hypothesized that language labels for the color spectrum are culturally idiosyncratic. These labels not only chop up the color continuum into purely conventional segments in every language community, but they probably do so differently in different language communities. By a series of ingenious experiments, Brown and Lenneberg (1954), Lenneberg (1953, 1957), Lantz and Stefflre (1964), and others have demonstrated that this is indeed true. They have demonstrated that those colors for which a language has readily available labels are more unhesitatingly named than are colors for which no such handy labels are available. They have shown that the colors for which a language has readily available labels (i.e., highly codable colors) are more readily recognized or remembered when they must be selected from among many colors after a delay subsequent to their initial presentation. They have demonstrated that somewhat different segments of the color spectrum are highly codable in different language communities. Finally, they have shown that the learning of nonsense-syllable associations for colors is predictably easier for highly codable colors than for less codable colors that require a phrase—often an individually formulated phrase—in order to be named.

All in all, this series of experiments has forcefully shown that the availability of a structured set of terms has both intralinguistic as well as interlinguistic consequences. However, in addition, it has underscored the equally important fact that every speech community has exactly the terms for those phenomena that are of concern to it. Certainly, artists, painters, and fashion buyers have a structured color terminology that goes far beyond that available to ordinary speakers of English. The relative absence or presence of particular color terms in the lexicon of a given speech network is thus not a reflection of the state of that network's *code per se* so much as it is a reflection of the color interests, sensitivities, and conventions of that network at a particular time in its history.

A color terminology is merely one kind of *folk taxonomy*, i.e., it is an example of the many *emic* semantic grids that are contained in the lexicons of all speech communities. Other such examples are the kinship terminologies of speech communities, their disease or illness terminologies, their plant terminologies, their terms of address, etc. (Basso 1967; Conklin 1962; Frake 1961, 1962; Pospisil 1965; Friederich 1966; Price 1967; Wittermans 1967; etc.). In each of these instances the particular lexicons involved constitute "un systeme où tout se tient." Each such system is considered by its users to be both literally exhaustive and objectively correct. Nevertheless, each system is socially particularistic, i.e., for all of its self-evident objectivity ("what other kind of kinship system could there *possibly* be?"—we can imagine the average member of each of the scores of such systems asking himself), it is a reflection of locally accepted conventions rather than a necessary reflection either of nature or of language per se. This last is particularly well demonstrated in the work of Friederich (on Russian kinship terms), Wittermans (on Javanese terms of address), and Basso (on Western Apache anatomical terms and their extension to auto parts; see Figure 8).

The Russian Revolution brought with it such fargoing social change that the kinship terms in use in Czarist days had to be changed to some degree. In contrast with the refined stratificational distinctions that existed in Czarist days— distinctions that recognized gradations of power, wealth, and proximity within the universe of kin, not unlike those that

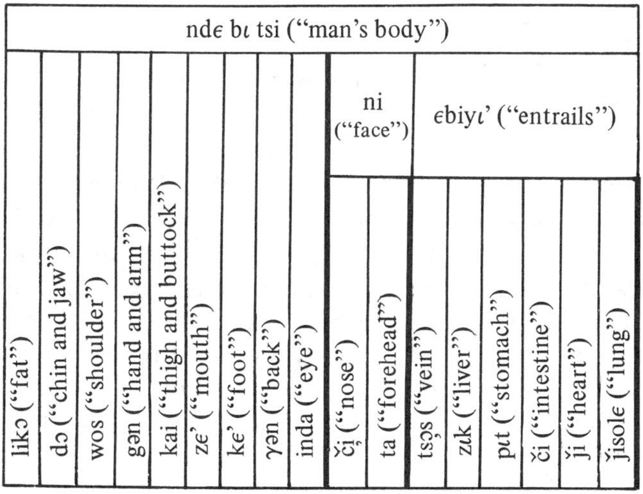

FIGURE 8A. Taxonomic Structure of Anatomical Set

Note: Black bars indicate position of additional (unextended) anatomical terms.

The chart shows nde bɩ tsi ("man's body") divided into terms: likɔ ("fat"), dɔ ("chin and jaw"), wos ("shoulder"), gən ("hand and arm"), kai ("thigh and buttock"), zɛ' ("mouth"), ke' ("foot"), ɣən ("back"), inda ("eye"), then ni ("face") comprising čįˀ ("nose"), ta ("forehead"), and ɛbiyɩ' ("entrails") comprising tsǫ́s ("vein"), zɩk ("liver"), pɩt ("stomach"), či ("intestine"), ǰi ("heart"), ǰisolɛ ("lung").

Western Apache

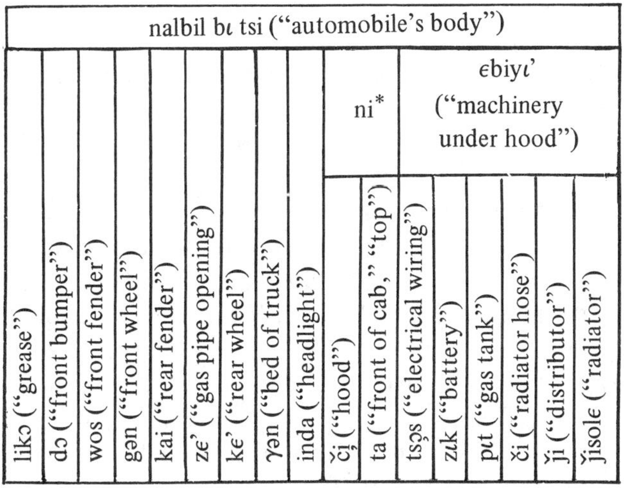

FIGURE 8B. Taxonomic Structure of Extended Set

*"Area extending from top of windshield to bumper"

The chart shows nalbil bɩ tsi ("automobile's body") divided into terms: likɔ ("grease"), dɔ ("front bumper"), wos ("front fender"), gən ("front wheel"), kai ("rear fender"), zɛ' ("gas pipe opening"), ke' ("rear wheel"), ɣən ("bed of truck"), inda ("headlight"), then ni* comprising čįˀ ("hood"), ta ("front of cab," "top"), and ɛbiyɩ' ("machinery under hood") comprising tsǫ́s ("electrical wiring"), zɩk ("battery"), pɩt ("gas tank"), či ("radiator hose"), ǰi ("distributor"), ǰisolɛ ("radiator").

Basso, Keith H., Semantic Aspects of Linguistic Acculturation, *American Anthropologist,* (1967), 69. 471-477.

were recognized in the larger universe of social and economic relationships—Soviet society stressed far fewer and broader distinctions. As a result, various kinship terms were abandoned entirely, others were merged and others were expanded. A very similar development occurred in Javanese with respect to its highly stratified system of terms of address. The impact of postwar independence, industrialization, urbanization, and the resulting modification or abandonment of traditional role relationships led to the discontinuation of certain terms of address and the broadening of others, particularly of those that implied relatively egalitarian status between interlocutors. Howell's review of changes in the pronouns of address in Japan (1967) also makes the same point, as did his earlier study of status markers in Korean (1965). Not only does he indicate how individuals change the pronouns that they use in referring to themselves and to each other, as their attitudes and roles vis-à-vis each other change, but he implies that widespread and cumulative changes of this kind have occurred in Japan since the war, with the result that certain pronouns have been practically replaced by others. Certainly the best known study of this kind is Brown and Gilman's review of widespread Western European social change with respect to the use of informal (T) vs. formal (V) pronouns and verb forms for the third person singular (1960). Feudalism, Renaissance, Reformation, the French Revolution, nineteenth-century liberalism, and twentieth-century democratization each had recognizable and cumulative impact. As a result, both T and V forms were retained in interclass communication (except in the case of English), but their differential use came to indicate differences primarily in *solidarity* or differences in *solidarity and in power* rather than differences in *power alone* as had been the case in the early Middle Ages (see Figure 9).

Note that the complexities of the prerevolutionary kinship taxonomies in Russia did not keep Russians from thinking about or from engaging in revolution. Note also that the revolution did not entirely scrap the pre-existing kinship

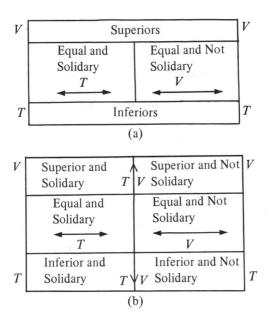

FIGURE 9. The two-dimensional semantic (a) in equilibrium and (b) under tension. (Brown and Gilman)

Solidarity comes into the European pronouns as a means of differentiating address among power equals. It introduces a second dimension into the semantic system on the level of power equivalents. So long as solidarity was confined to this level, the two-dimensional system was in equilibrium (see Figure 1a), and it seems to have remained here for a considerable time in all our languages. It is from the long reign of the two-dimensional semantic that *T* derives its common definition as the pronoun of either condescension or intimacy and *V* its definition as the pronoun of reverence or formality. These definitions are still current but usage has, in fact, gone somewhat beyond them.

The dimension of solidarity is potentially applicable to all persons addressed. Power superiors may be solidary (parents, elder siblings) or not solidary (officials whom one seldom sees). Power inferiors, similarly, may be as solidary as the old family retainer and as remote as the waiter in a strange restaurant. Extension of the solidarity dimension along the dotted lines of Figure 1b creates six categories of persons defined by their relations to a speaker. Rules of address are in conflict for persons in the upper left and lower right categories. For the upper left, power indicates *V* and solidarity *T*. For the lower right, power indicates *T* and solidarity *V*.

Well into the nineteenth century the power semantic prevailed and waiters, common soldiers, and employees were called *T* while parents, masters, and elder brothers were called *V*. However, all our evidence consistently indicates that in the past century the solidarity semantic has gained supremacy. The abstract result is a simple one-dimensional system with the reciprocal *T* for the solidary and the reciprocal *V* for the nonsolidary.

taxonomy. Similarly, the Apache anatomical taxonomy did not preclude (but rather assisted) taxonomic organization of automobile parts. Thus, while we are clearly indicating the untenability of any strong linguistic *relativity* position when we show that semantic taxonomies are subject to change, expansion, and contraction as the sociocultural realities of their users change, we are also demonstrating that their linguistic *reflection* of social reality is also likely to be both slow and partial. Nevertheless, as between the two, the taxonomic *reflection* of sociocultural reality is more likely to have widespread heuristic utility at any given time, however much the existence of such taxonomies is likely to be *constraining* in the momentary cognitive behavior of individual members of sociocultural systems.

The *emic* distinctions which underlie these taxonomies are differentially constraining for various interaction networks within any speech community. Some networks (e.g., the networks of quantitative scientists) can repeatedly rise above the cognitive constraints of the taxonomies current in their speech communities. These networks are likely to be the ones that are most actively engaged in social change and in taxonomic change as well. Other networks are unable to break out of the sociocultural taxonomies that surround them. In such cases as, e.g., in connection with Kantrowitz' race relations taxonomy among white and Negro prison inmates (1967; see Figure 10), or Price's botanical taxonomies among the Huichols (1967), these taxonomies may be taken not only as useful *reflections* of the cognitive world of the speech community from which they were derived, but also as forceful *constraints* on the cognitive behavior of most, if not all, of the individual members of these networks.

6.3 LEXICAL STRUCTURE REFLECTS SOCIAL ORGANIZATION

There are, however, more pervasive (and, therefore, seemingly less systematic) ways in which lexicons in particular and

FIGURE 10. Selected Examples of Vocabulary Used by White and Negro Prison Inmates

CONCEPTS OR *names* USED EXCLUSIVELY BY NEGROES	*names* USED IN COMMON BY BOTH NEGROES AND WHITES	CONCEPTS OR *names* USED EXCLUSIVELY BY WHITES
A white man who does not discriminate against Negroes		A white man who associates with Negroes
↓		↓
free thinker		*nigger lover*
A Negro who believes whites are superior, and acts subservient to them		A Negro who is not aggressive or does not insist on his equal rights with whites
↓	*sander, smoke-blower, easy going-black slave*	↓
jeff, jeffer, jeff-davis, jeff artist, charlie mccarthy, chalk eyes, renegade, shuffler, sometimer, uncle tom, devil lover, stays in uncle tom's-cabin, hoosier lover		*free thinker*
A Negro who constantly tells both Negroes and whites that Negroes must be accorded the same status and rights as whites		A Negro who hates whites, and expresses it vehemently and freely among Negroes
↓	*civil rights man, race man, mau mau, equal rights man*	↓
aggressive man, free-speaker, man of-reasoning		*civil rights nigger, freedom rider, little-rocker, lumumba, a-martin luther king, mau mau preacher, muslim, pale hater, tom tom guy*

N. Kantrowitz, ADS, Chicago, (1967).

languages as a whole are reflective of the speech communities that employ them. In a very real sense a language variety is an inventory of the concerns and interests of those who employ it at any given time. If any portion of this inventory reveals features not present in other portions, this may be indicative of particular stresses or influences in certain interaction networks within the speech community as a whole or in certain role relationships within the community's total role repertoire. Thus Epstein's study of linguistic innovation on the Copperbelt of Northern Rhodesia (1959) revealed that the English and other Western influences on the local languages were largely limited to matters dealing with urban, industrial, and generally nontraditional pursuits and relationships. Similarly, M. Weinreich's meticulous inquiry into the non-Germanic elements in Yiddish (1953) sheds much light on the dynamics of German-Jewish relations in the eleventh-century Rhineland.

Like all other immigrants to differently speaking milieus, Jews, learning a variety of medieval German in the eleventh century, brought to this language-learning task sociolinguistic norms which incorporated their prior verbal repertoire. In this case the repertoire consisted of a vernacular (Loez, a variety of Romance) and a set of sacred languages (Hebrew-Aramaic). However, the pre-existing sociolinguistic norms did not impinge upon the newly acquired Germanic code either in a random fashion or on an equal-sampling basis. Quite the contrary. Both the Romance and the Hebraic-Aramaic elements in Yiddish were overwhelmingly retained to deal with a specific domain: traditional religious pursuits and concerns. The Christological overtones of many common German words, for example *lesen* (to read) and *segnen* (to bless), were strong enough to lead to the retention of more neutral words of Romance origin (*leyenen* and *bentshn*) in their stead. Similarly, Hebrew and Aramaic terms were retained not only for all traditional and sanctified objects and ceremonies, but also in doublets with certain Germanic elements in order to provide contrastive emphases: *bukh* (book) vs. *séyfer* (religious book, scholarly book); *lerer* (teacher) vs. *melámed* or *rébi* (teacher of religious subjects), etc. Thus Yiddish is a wonderful example of how *all* languages in contact borrow from each other selectively and of how this very selectivity is indicative of the primary interests and emphases of the borrowers and the donors alike. Indeed, M. Weinreich has conclusively demonstrated (1953, 1967, etc.) that a language not only reflects the society of its speakers, but conversely that societal data per se is crucial if language usage and change are to be understood.

Section VII

APPLIED SOCIOLINGUISTICS

One of the wisest maxims that Kurt Lewin bequeathed to social psychology is that which claims that "nothing is as practical as a good theory." In addition, social science theory is undoubtedly enriched by attempting to cope with the real problems of the workaday world. Thus if social science theory is *really* any good (really powerful, really correct) it should have relevance for practitioners whose work brings them into contact with larger or smaller groups of human beings. Applied sociolinguistics attempts both to enrich sociolinguistics and to assist in the solution of societal language problems. Applied sociolinguistics is of particular interest whenever: (a) language varieties must be "developed" in order to function in the vastly new settings, role relationships, or purposes in which certain important networks of their speakers come to be involved, or (b) whenever important networks of a speech community must be taught varieties that they do not know well (or at all), so that they may function in the vastly new settings, role relationships, or purposes that might then be open to them. In many instances (a) and (b) co-occur, that is, language varieties must be both developed and taught in order that import networks within a speech community may be fruitfully involved in the new settings, role relationships, and purposes that have become available to them. This is but another way of saying that planned language change and planned social change are highly interrelated activities and that applied sociolinguistics is pertinent to their interaction.

7.1 THE FORMULATION OF LANGUAGE POLICY

Applied sociolinguistics most often comes into play when decisions concerning language policy have been reached and require implementation. It is to be hoped that as language planning and social-planning agencies become more aware of the possible contributions of applied sociolinguistics, they may become more inclined to involve sociolinguists and other language specialists in guiding the decision-making process itself rather than merely in implementing decisions already reached. Several signs already point in this direction. Thus the several nations of East Africa are interested in the current "Survey of Language Use and Language Teaching" (Prator 1967) in order to adopt (or revise) language operations in schools, mass media, public services, etc., on the basis of more precise information as to the age, number, location, and interactions of the speakers of various local languages. Similarly, the Philippine government has long followed a policy of evaluating language policy in the area of education via research projects dealing with such matters as the advisability of initiating education in the local mother tongues and introducing the national language (Tagalog) only in some optimal subsequent year (Ramos et al. 1967). The Irish government has sponsored "motivation research" and opinion polls in order to determine how its citizens view the Irish language and how they react to the government's efforts to "restore" it to wider functions (Anon. 1968). One of the most widely cited guides to governmental language policies and their educational implications is an applied sociolinguistic report issued by UNESCO and dealing with *The Use of the Vernacular in Education* (Anon. 1953).

7.2 THE IMPLEMENTATION OF LANGUAGE POLICY

Once a policy has been adopted it is then necessary to implement it. Such implementation not only takes the obvious route of requiring and/or encouraging the functional reallocation of varieties, but also their phonological, lexical, and grammatical realization along prescribed lines. Language agencies, institutes, academies, or boards are commonly authorized to develop or plan the variety selected by policy makers. Such agencies are increasingly likely to seek feedback concerning the effectiveness or the acceptability of the "products" (orthographies, dictionaries, grammars, spellers, textbooks, translation series, subsidized literary works, etc.) that they have produced. Sociolinguists have already produced many studies which language agencies are likely to find extremely useful in terms of their implications for the work that such agencies conduct.

The studies by Berry (1958), Sjoberg (1966), Smalley (1964) and Stern (1968) are likely to be of great value in planning alphabets for hitherto nonliterate peoples whose languages are destined to become vehicles of literacy. The difficulties cenountered and the lessons learned in planned lexical expansion to cope with the terminology of modern technology, education, government, and daily life are recounted by Alisjabana (1962), Bacon (1966), Morag (1959), Passin (1963), and Tietze (1962) in their accounts of language planning in Indonesia, Central Asia, Japan, Israel, and Turkey, respectively. The problems of planned language standardization have been illuminated by Ferguson (1968), Garvin (1959), Guxman (1960), Ray (1963), U. Weinreich (1953), Havranek (1958), Valdman (1968), and Twadell (1959) in sufficiently general terms to be of interest in any speech community where this process needs to be set in motion.

7.3 LANGUAGE PLANNING

Even the very process of government involvement in language issues has begun to be documented. In this connection one must mention the reports of the Irish government on its own efforts to restore the Irish language (Anon. 1965); Goodman's review of Soviet efforts to provide—as well as to deny—indigenous *standard* languages to the peoples under their control (Goodman 1960); Haugen's many insightful reports of the Norwegian government's attempts to cope with language conflict by both protecting and limiting the linguistic divergence of its citizenry (Haugen 1961, 1966a, 1966b); Heyd's account of language reform in modern Turkey (Heyd 1954); Lunt's account of the studied efforts in Titoist Yugoslavia to separate Macedonian from Serbian and from Bulgarian (Lunt 1959); the contrasts between different parts of Africa noted by Armstrong (1968), Polome (1968), and Whiteley (1968); Mills's report of how Communist China advanced and retreated in connection with the writing reform it so desperately needs (Mills 1956); Wurm's descriptions of the very beginnings of language policy in reference to Pidgin English ("Neomelanesian") in New Guinea (Wurm and Laycock 1961-1962), and several others (e.g., Brosnahan 1963; LePage 1964; Fishman 1968c) of more general or conceptual relevance.

7.4 EDUCATIONAL APPLICATIONS

One of the most developed areas of applied sociolinguistics is that which deals with educational problems. In this connection there have been studies of the organization and operation of bilingual schools (Gaarder 1967); of the academic consequences of compulsory education via the weaker language for most learners (Macnamara 1966, 1967); of different approaches to teaching hitherto untaught mother tongues (Davis 1967); of varying South American and West Indian approaches to teaching both local and "wider" languages (Burns 1968; LePage 1968; Rubin 1968); of difficulties in teaching English (as the compulsory school language for non-English speakers) encountered by teachers who are themselves nonnative speakers of English (Lanham 1965); and, more specifically, of the problem of teaching standard English to speakers of very discrepant, nonstandard varieties of that language (Stewart 1964, 1965). A more generalized interest in applied sociolinguistics is that shown by the recent Canadian Royal Commission on Bilingualism and Biculturism. It authorized studies not only of bilingual schooling, but also of bilingualism in broadcasting, in industrial operations, in military operations, and in the operation of various other social enterprises.

7.5 THE RATIONALIZATION OF LANGUAGE DECISION

All in all, applied sociolinguistics has been concerned with (a) providing information on the basis of which language policy could be tentatively or experimentally formulated, (b) experimenting with small-scale alternative approaches to language policy, (c) determining the political and other intergroup and interpersonal processes via which language decisions are reached, (d) studying the consequences of language policy in terms of the authoritative implementation of policy, and (e) studying the consequences of language policy in terms of target-population responses to the programs or products that have been devised by authoritative bodies. In the near future we may also expect attemts at cost/benefit analysis of various sociolinguistic policies. Given such analyses the costs of alternative policies may become more apparent and, in some instances, may even become predictable. Language planning as a rational and technical process informed by actuarial data and by ongoing feedback is still a dream, but it is by no means so farfetched a dream as it seemed to be merely a decade ago.

At the present time, sociolinguistics is largely a descriptive science. Given further advances in applied sociolinguistics and continued interaction between theory and application, sociolinguistics may well become a far more experimental discipline in the future than it has been in the past (Ervin-Tripp 1968). Undergraduate and graduate training in sociolinguistics, now just beginning primarily under the impetus of the Social Science Research Council's "Committee on Sociolinguistics," will certainly increase rapidly in the future, particularly as experimental and applied sociolinguistic research and research opportunities grow in number and in importance.

DR. FERGUSON'S REFERENCES

Bright, William (ed.), *Sociolinguistics*. Mouton, The Hague, 1966.

Brown, Roger W. and Albert Gilman. "The Pronouns of Power and Solidarity," in T. A. Seboek (ed.), *Style in Language*. MIT Press and Wiley, Cambridge and New York, 1960, pp. 253-276.

Ervin-Tripp, Susan M. "Sociolinguistics," in L. Berkowitz (ed.), *Advances in Experimental Social Psychology* Vol. 4. Academic Press, New York, 1969, pp. 91-165.

Fishman, Joshua A. et al. *Language Loyalty in the United States.* Mouton, The Hague, 1966.

Fishman, Joshua A. *Readings in the Sociology of Language.* Mouton, The Hague, 1968.

Fishman, Joshua A., Robert L. Cooper, Roxana Ma, et al. *Bilingualism in the Barrio.* Report to the U.S. Office of Education. 2 vols. New York: Yeshiva University, 1968, in press, Indiana University Press.

Fishman, Joshua A., Charles A. Ferguson, and Jyotindra Das Gupta, (eds.), *Language Problems of Developing Nations.* Wiley, New York, 1968.

Grimshaw, Allan W. "Sociolinguistics," in Wilbur Schramm et al (eds.), *Handbook of Communication.* Rand-McNally, Chicago, in press.

Gumperz, John J. "Language and Communication," *The Annals* 1967, pp. 219-231, 373.

Hymes, Dell (ed.). *Language in Culture and Society.* Harper, New York, 1967.

Hymes, Dell and John J. Gumperz (eds.), *Ethnography of Communication (American Anthropologist* 66:2, 1964).

Labov, William. "Phonological Correlates of Social Stratification," in Hymes and Gumperz (eds.), *Ethnography of Communication, (American Anthropologist* 66:2, 1964), pp. 164-176.

BIBLIOGRAPHY

Alisjahbana, S, Takdir. "The Modernization of the Indonesian Language in Practice," in his *Indonesian Language and Literature: Two Essays.* Yale University Southeast Asia Studies, New Haven, Conn., 1962, pp. 1-22.

Anon. *The Use of Vernacular Languages in Education.* UNESCO, Paris, 1953.

_____. *The Restoration of the Irish Language.* Ministry of Finance, Dublin, 1965.

_____. *A Motivational Research Study for the Greater Use of the Irish Language,* 2 vols. Ernest Dichter International Institute for Motivational Research, Croton-on-Hudson, N.Y., 1968.

Armstrong, Robert. "Language Policies and Language Practices in West Africa," in Fishman, J. A., C. A. Ferguson, and J. Das Gupta (eds.), *Language Problems of Developing Nations.* Wiley, New York, 1968.

Bacon, Elizabeth E. Russian Influence on Central Asian Languages," in her *Central Asians under Russian Rule.* Cornell, Ithaca, N.Y., 1966.

Barker, George C. "Social Functions of Language in a Mexican-American Community," *Acta Americana,* V (1947), 185-202.

Basso, Keith H. "Semantic Aspects of Linguistic Acculturation," *American Anthropologist,* LXIX (1967), 471-477.

Bell, Daniel. *The End of Ideology.* Collier, New York, 1961.

Bernstein, Basil. "Elaborated and Restricted Codes: Their Social Origins and Some Consequences," *American Anthropologist,* LXVI, ii (1964), 37-53.

———. "Elaborated and Restricted Codes: An Outline," *Sociological Inquiry,* XXXVI (1966), 254-261.

Berry, Jack. "The Making of Alphabets," *Proceedings of the Eighth International Congress of Linguistics.* Oslo University Press, Oslo, 1958, pp. 752-764.

Blanc, Haim. *Communal Dialects in Baghdad.* Harvard, Cambridge, Mass., 1964.

Blom, Jan Peter, and John J. Gumperz. "Some Social Determinants of Verbal Behavior," in John J. Gumperz and Dell Hymes (eds.), *The Ethnography of Communication: Directions in Sociolinguistics.* Holt, New York, 1971.

Bloomfield, Leonard. *Language.* Holt, New York, 1933.

Bock, Philip K. "Social Structure and Language Structure," *Southwestern Journal of Anthropology,* XX (1964), 393-403. (Also in J. A. Fishman (ed.), *Readings,* pp. 212-222.)

Bonjean, Charles M. "Mass, Class and the Industrial Community: A Comparative Analysis of Managers, Businessmen and Workers," *American Journal of Sociology,* LXXII (1966), 149-162.

Boulding, Kenneth. "The Death of the City: A Frightened Look at Post Civilization," in Oscar Handlin, and John Burchard (eds.), *The Historian and the City.* MIT and Harvard, Cambridge, Mass., 1963, p. 145.

Broom, Leonard, and Norval D. Glenn. "Negro-White Differences in Reported Attitudes and Behavior," *Sociology and Social Research,* L (1966), 187-200.

Brosnahan, L. F. "Some Historical Cases of Language Imposition," in Robert Spencer (ed.), *Language in Africa.* Cambridge University Press, London, 1963, pp. 7-24.

Brown, Roger W., and Albert Gilman. "The Pronouns of Power and Solidarity," in Thomas A. Sebeok (ed.), *Style in Language.* MIT, Cambridge, Mass., and Wiley, New York, 1960, pp. 253-276. (Also in J. A. Fishman (ed.), *Readings,* pp. 252-275.

———, and Eric H. Lenneberg. "A Study in Language and Cognition," *J. Abnorm. Soc. Psychol.,* XLIX (1954, 454-462.

Burns, Robert. "Bilingual Education in the Andes of Peru," in J. A. Fishman, C. A. Ferguson, and J. Das Gupta (eds.), *Language Problems of the Developing Nations.* Wiley, New York, 1968.

Carmichael, L., H. P. Hogan, and A. A. Walter. "An Experimental Study of the Effect of Language on the Perception of Visually Perceived Form," *J. Exp. Psychol.*, XV (1932), 73-86.

Carroll, John B., and J. B. Casagrande. "The Function of Language Classifications in Behavior," in E. Maccoby, T. Newcomb, and E. Hartley (eds.), *Readings in Social Psychology.* Holt, New York, 1958, pp. 18-31.

Chomsky, Noam. *Syntactic Structures.* Mouton, The Hague, 1957.

_____. *Aspects of a Theory of Syntax.* MIT, Cambridge, Mass., 1965.

Conklin, Harold C. Lexicographical Treatment of Folk Taxonomies," in Fred W. Householder and Sol Saporta (eds.), *Problems in Lexicography.* Indiana Univ. Research Center in Anthropology, Folklore and Linguistics, Publication 21, Bloomington, 1962, pp. 119-141.

Davis, Frederick B. *Philippine Language-Teaching Experiments* (Philippine Center for Language Study, no. 5). Alemar-Phoenix, Quezon City, 1967.

de Saussure, Ferdinand. *Course in General Linguistics* (translated by Wade Baskin). Philosophical Library, New York, 1959. (French original: 1916)

Deutsch, Karl W. *Nationalism and Social Communication,* 2nd ed. MIT, Cambridge, Mass., 1966.

Epstein, A. L. "Linguistic Innovation and Culture on the Copperbelt, Northern Rhodesia," *Southwestern Journal of Anthropology,* XV (1959), 235-253. (Also in J. A. Fishman (ed.), *Readings,* pp. 320-339.)

Ervin-Tripp, Susan M. "An Analysis of the Interaction between Language, Topic, and Speaker," *American Anthropologist,* LXVI, ii (1964), 86-102. (Also in J. A. Fishman (ed.), *Readings,* pp. 192-211.)

_____. "Sociolinguistics," in L. Berkowitz (ed.), *Advances in Experimental Social Psychology,* vol. 4. Academic Press, New York, 1968.

Ferguson, Charles A. "Diglossia," *Word,* XV (1959a), 325-340.

_____. "Myths about Arabic," *Monograph Series on Languages and Linguistics (Georgetown University),* 12, 1959b, 75-82. (Also in J. A. Fishman (ed.), *Readings,* pp. 375-381.)

_____. "Language Development," in J. A. Fishman, C. A. Ferguson, and J. Das Gupta (eds.), *Language Problems of the Developing Nations.* Wiley, New York, 1968

_____, and John J. Gumperz (eds.), "Linguistic Diversity in South Asia: Studies in Regional, Social, and Functional Variation," *International Journal of American Linguistics,* IV, i (1960) (entire issue).

Fischer, John L. "Social Influences on the Choice of a Linguistic Variant," *Word,* XIV (1958), 47-56.

Fishman, Joshua A. "A Systematization of the Whorfian Hypothesis," *Behavioral Science,* VIII (1960), 323-339.

_____. "Language Maintenance and Language Shift as Fields of Inquiry," *Linguistics,* IX (1964), 32-70.

_____. *Yiddish in America.* Indiana University Research Center in Anthropology, Folklore and Linguistics, Publication 36, Bloomington, 1965a.

_____. "Bilingualism, Intelligence, and Language Learning," *Modern Language Journal,* XLIX (1965b), 227-237.

_____. "Varieties of Ethnicity and Language Consciousness," *Monograph Series on Languages and Linguistics (Georgetown Univ.),* XVIII (1965c), 69-79.

_____. "Who Speaks What Language to Whom and When?" *Linguistique,* II (1965d), 67-88.

_____. "Language Maintenance and Language Shift; the American Immigrant Case within a General Theoretical Perspective," *Sociologus,* XVI (1965e), 19-38.

_____. "Bilingual Sequences at the Societal Level," *On Teaching English to Speakers of Other Languages,* II (1966a), 139-144.

_____. "Some Contrasts between Linguistically Homogeneous and Linguistically Heterogeneous Polities." *Sociological Inquiry,* XXXVI (1966b), 146-158. (Revised and expanded in J. A. Fishman, C. A. Ferguson, and J. Das Gupta [eds.], *Language Problems of the Developing Nations.* Wiley, New York, 1968.

_____. *Language Loyalty in the United States.* Mouton, The Hague, 1966c.

_____. "The Breadth and Depth of English in the United States," *University Quarterly,* March, 1967, 133-140.

_____. *Readings in the Sociology of Language.* Mouton, The Hague, 1968a.

_____. "Sociolinguistic Perspective on the Study of Bilingualism," *Linguistics,* XXXIX (1968b), 21-50.

_____. "Sociolinguistics and the Language Problems of Developing Nations," *International Social Science Journal,* XXX (1968c) 211-222.

_____. "The Links between Micro and Macro Sociolinguistics in the Study of Who Speaks What Language to Whom and When," in Dell Hymes and John J. Gumperz (eds.), *The Ethnography of Communication: Directions in Sociolinguistics.* Holt, New York, 1971.

_____. Robert L. Cooper, Roxana Ma, *et al. Bilingualism in the Barrio.* Final Report on Contract OEC-1-7-062817-0297 to DHEW. Yeshiva University, New York, 1968.

Frake, Charles. "The Diagnosis of Disease among the Sibanun of Mindanao," *American Anthropologist,* LXIII 1961, 113-132.

_____. The Ethnographic Study of Cognitive Systems, in T. Gladwin and William C. Sturtevant (eds.), *Anthropology and Behavior.* Anthropological Society of Washington, Washington, D.C., 1962, pp. 77-85. (Also in J. A. Fishman [ed.], *Readings,* pp. 434-466.)

Friederich, Paul. "The Linguistic Reflex of Social Change: From Tsarist to Soviet Russian Kinship," *Sociological Inquiry,* XXXVI (1966), 159-185.

_____. "Language and Politics in India," *Daedalus,* Summer, 1962, 543-559.

Gaarder, Bruce. "Organization of the Bilingual School," *Journal of Social Issues,* XXIII (1967), 110-120.

Garfinkel, Harold. *Studies in Ethnomethodology.* Prentice-Hall, Englewood Cliffs, N.J., 1967.

_____, and H. Sacks (eds.), *Contributions in Ethnomethodology.* Indiana University Press, Bloomington, in press.

Garvin, Paul. "The Standard Language Problem: Concepts and Methods," *Anthropological Linguistics,* I, ii (1959), 28-31.

Geertz, Clifford. "Linguistic Etiquette," in his *Religion of Java.* Glencoe Press, New York, 1960. (Also in J. A. Fishman [ed.], *Readings,* pp. 282-295.)

Glenn, Norval D. "The Trend in Differences in Attitudes and Behavior by Educational Level," *Sociology of Education,* XXXIX (1966), 255-275.

_____, and J. L. Simmons. "Are Regional Cultural Differences Diminishing?" *Public Opinion Quarterly,* XXXI (1967a), 176-193.

_____. Differentiation and Massification: Some Trend Data from National Surveys. *Social Forces,* XLVI (1967b), 172-179.

Goodenough, Ward H. "Rethinking 'Status' and 'Role': Toward a General Model of the Cultural Organization of Social Relationships," in M. Banton (ed.), *The Relevance of Models for Social Anthropology.* Praeger, New York, 1965, pp. 1-24.

Goodman, Elliot R. "World State and World Language," in his *The Soviet Design for a World State.* Columbia, New York, 1960, pp. 264-284. (Also in J. A. Fishman [ed.], *Readings,* pp. 717-736.)

Greenberg, Joseph R. *Universals of Language,* 2nd ed. MIT, Cambridge, Mass., 1966.

_____. Urbanism, Migration, and Language, in Kuper, Hilda (ed.), *Urbanization and Migration in West Africa*. Univ. of Calif. Press, (1965), 50-59.

Gumperz, John J. "Dialect Differences and Social Stratification in a North Indian Village," *American Anthropologist,* LX (1958), 668-682.

_____. "Speech Variation and the Study of Indian Civilization," *American Anthropologist,* LXIII (1961), 976-988.

_____. "Types of Linguistic Communities," *Anthropological Linguistics,* IV, i (1962) 28-40. (Also in J. A. Fishman [ed.] , *Readings,* pp. 460-472.)

_____. "Linguistic and Social Interaction in Two Communities," *American Anthropologist,* LXVI, ii (1964a), 37-53.

_____. "Hindi-Punjabi Code Switching in Delhi," in Morris Halle (ed.), *Proceedings of the International Congress of Linguistics.* Mouton, The Hague, 1964b.

_____. "On the Ethnology of Linguistic Change," in William Bright, (ed.), *Sociolinguistics.* Mouton, The Hague, 1966, pp. 27-38.

_____. The Linguistic Markers of Bilingualism. *Journal of Social Issues,* XXIII, ii (1967), 48-57.

Guxman, M. M. "Some General Regularities in the Formation and Development of National Languages," in M. M. Guxman (ed.), *Voprosy Formirovanija i Razvitija Nacional'nyx Jazykov.* Moscow, 1960, pp. 295-307. (Also in J. A. Fishman [ed.] *Readings,* pp. 766-779.)

Halliday, M. A. K. "The Users and Uses of Language," in M. A. K. Halliday, A. McIntosh, and P. Stevens (eds.), *The Linguistic Sciences and Language Teaching.* Longmans, London, 1964. (Also in J. A. Fishman (ed.), *Readings,* pp. 139-169.)

Hamilton, Richard F. "Affluence and the Worker: The West German Case," *American Journal of Sociology,* LXXI (1965), 144-152.

Haugen, Einar. Language Planning in Modern Norway. *Scandinavian Studies.* XXXI, (1961), 68-81. (Also in J. A. Fishman (ed.), *Readings,* pp. 673-687.)

_____. *Language Planning and Language Conflict; The Case of Modern Norwegian.* Harvard, Cambridge, Mass., 1966a.

_____. "Linguistics and Language Planning," in William Bright (ed.), *Sociolinguistics.* Mouton, The Hague, 1966b, pp. 50-66.

_____. Dialect, Language, Nation. *American Anthropologist,* LXVIII (1966c), 922-935.

Havranek, Bohuslav. "The Functional Differentiation of the Standard Language," in Paul L. Garvin (ed.), *A Prague School Reader on*

Esthetics, Literary Structure and Style. Washington, D.C., 1964, pp. 1-18.

Herman, Simon N. "Explorations in the Social Psychology of Language Choice," *Human Relations,* XIV (1961), 149-164. (Also in J. A. Fishman (ed.), *Readings,* pp. 492-511.)

Hertzler, Joyce O. *The Sociology of Language,* Random House, New York, 1965.

Herzog, Marvin I. *The Yiddish Language in Northern Poland: Its Geography and History.* Indiana University Press, Bloomington, 1965.

Heyd, Uriel. *Language Reform in Modern Turkey.* Israel Oriental Society, Jerusalem, 1954.

Hodges, Harold M. *Social Stratification: Class in America.* Schenkman, Cambridge, Mass., 1964.

Hoijer, H. "Cultural Implications of the Navaho Linguistic Categories," *Language,* XXVII (1951), 111-120.

_____. "The Sapir-Whorf Hypothesis," in H. Hoijer (ed.), *Language in Culture.* American Anthropological Association, Memoir 79, 92-104, 1954.

Howell, Richard W. Linguistic Status Markers in Korean. *Kroeber Anthropological Society Papers,* LV (1965), 91-97.

_____. "Terms of Address as Indices of Social Change." Paper presented at American Sociological Association Meeting, San Francisco, Sept., 1967.

Hymes, Dell. "The Ethnography of Speaking," in T. Gladwin and William C. Sturtevant (eds.), *Anthropology and Human Behavior.* Anthrop. Soc. of Wash., Washington, 1962, pp. 13-53. (Also in J. A. Fishman [ed.], *Readings,* pp. 99-138.)

_____. "Two Types of Linguistic Relativity," in William Bright (ed.), *Sociolinguistics.* Mouton, The Hague, 1966, pp. 114-157.

_____. "Models of the Interaction of Language and Social Setting," *Journal of Social Issues,* XXIII, ii (1967), 8-28.

Joos, Martin. "The Isolation of Styles," *Monograph Series on Languages and Linguistics (Georgetown University),* XII (1959), 107-113. (Also in J. A. Fishman [ed.], *Readings,* pp. 185-191.)

Kantrowitz, Nathan. "The Vocabulary of Race Relations in a Prison." Paper presented at American Dialect Society Meeting, Chicago, December, 1967.

Kloss, Heinz. *Die Entwicklung neuer germanischer Kultursprachen.* Pohl, Munich, 1952.

_____. "Types of Multilingual Communities: A Discussion of Ten Variables," *Sociological Inquiry,* XXXVI (1966), 36, 135-145.

_____. " 'Abstand languages' and 'Ausbau languages.' "*Anthropological Linguistics,* IX, vii (1967), 29-41.

Kluckhohn, Clyde. "Notes on Some Anthropological Aspects of Communication," *American Anthropologist,* LXIII (1961), 895-910.

Labov, William. "The Social Motivation of a Sound Change," *Word,* XIX (1963), 273-309.

_____. "Phonological Correlates of Social Stratification," *American Anthropologist,* LXVI, ii (1964), 164-176.

_____. "On the Mechanism of Linguistic Change," *Monograph Series in Languages and Linguistics (Georgetown University),* XVIII (1965), 91-114.

_____. "The Effect of Social Mobility on Linguistic Behavior," *Sociological Inquiry,* XXXVI (1966a), 186-203.

_____. "Hypercorrection by the Lower Middle Class as a Factor in Linguistic Change," in William Bright (ed.), *Sociolinguistics.* Mouton, The Hague, 1966b, pp. 84-101.

_____. "The Reflection of Social Processes in Linguistic Structures," in J. A. Fishman (ed.), *Readings in the Sociology of Language.* Mouton, The Hague, 1968, pp. 240-251.

Lanham, L. W. "Teaching English to Africans: A Crisis in Education," *Optima,* V (Dec., 1965), 197-204.

Lantz, De Lee, and Volney Stefflre. "Language and Cognition Revisited," *J. Abnorm. Soc. Psychol.,* XLIX (1964), 454-462.

Lehmann, A. *"Uber Wiedererkennen,"* Philos. Stud.,V (1889), 96-156.

Lenneberg, Eric H. "Cognition in Ethnolinguistics," *Language,* XXIX (1953), 463-471.

_____. "A Probabilistic Approach to Language Learning," *Behavioral Science,* II (1957), 1-12.

LePage, Robert. *The National Language Question.* Oxford Univ. Press, London, 1964.

_____. "Problems to Be Faced in the Use of English as the Medium of Education in Four West Indian Territories," in J. A. Fishman, C. A. Ferguson, and J. Das Gupta (eds.), *Language Problems of the Developing Nations.* Wiley, New York, 1968.

Levine, William L., and H. J. Crockett. "Speech Variation in a Piedmont Community: Postvocalic r." *Sociological Inquiry,* XXXVI (1966), 204-226.

Lieberson, Stanley. "Bilingualism in Montreal: A Demographic Analysis," *American Journal of Sociology,* LXXI (1965), 10-25.

Lunt, Horace G. "The Creation of Standard Macedonian: Some Facts and Attitudes," *Anthropological Linguistics*, I, v (1959), 19-26.

Macnamara, John. *Bilingualism in Primary Education.* Edinburgh University Press, Edinburgh, 1966.

_____. "The Effects of Instruction in a Weaker Language," *Journal of Social Issues*, XXIII (1967), 121-135.

Maier, Norman R. F. "Reasoning in Humans. I. On Direction," *J. Comp. Psychol.*, X (1930), 115-143.

McCormack, William. "Social Dialects in Dharwar Kannada," in C. A. Ferguson and J. J. Gumperz (eds.), *Linguistic Diversity in South Asia. IJAL*, IV, i (1960), 79-91.

Mills, H. C. Language Reform in China. *Far Eastern Quarterly*, XV (1956), 517-540.

Morag, Shelomo. "Planned and Unplanned Development in Modern Hebrew," *Lingua*, LXXXVII (1959), 247-263.

Nader, Laura. A Note on Attitudes and the Use of Language. *Anthropological Linguistics*, IV, vi (1962), 25-29.

Nahirny, Vladimir C., and Joshua A. Fishman, "American Immigrant Groups: Ethnic Identification and the Problem of Generations," *Sociological Review*, XIII (1965), 311-326.

Osgood, Charles E. "The Cross-Cultural Generality of Visual-Verbal Synesthetic Tendencies," *Behavioral Science*, V (1960), 146-169.

Owens, Roger C. "The Patrilocal Band: A Linguistically and Culturally Hybrid Social Unit," *American Anthropologist*, LXVII (1965), 675-690.

Passin, Herbert. "Writer and Journalist in the Transitional Society," in Lucian W. Pye (ed.), *Communication and Political Development.* Princeton, Princeton, N.J., 1963, pp. 82-123. (Also in J. A. Fishman, C. A. Ferguson, and J. Das Gupta [eds.], *Language Problems of the Developing Nations.* Wiley, New York, 1968.

Polome, Edgar. "The Choice of Official Languages in the Democratic Republic of the Congo," in J. A. Fishman, C. A. Ferguson, and J. Das Gupta (eds.), *Language Problems of Developing Countries.* Wiley, New York, 1968.

Pospisil, Leopold. "A Formal Semantic Analysis of Substantive Law: Kapauka Papuan Laws of Land Tenure," *American Anthropologist*, LXVII, pt. 2 (1965), 186-214.

Prator, Clifford H. "The Survey of Language Use and Language Teaching in Eastern Africa," *Linguistic Reporter*, IX, viii (1967).

Price, P. David. "Two Types of Taxonomy: A Huichol Ethnobotanical Example," *Anthropological Linguistics*, IX, vii (1967), 1-28.

Ramos, Maximo, Jose V. Aguilar, and Bonifacio P. Sibayan, *The Determination and Implementation of Language Policy* (Philippine Center for Language Study, Monograph 2). Alemar-Phoenix, Quezon City, 1967.

Ray, Punya Sloka. *Language Standardization*. Mouton, The Hague, 1963.

Ross, Allan S. C. "U and non-U; an Essay in Sociological Linguistics," in N. Mitford (ed.), *Noblesse Oblige*. Hamish Hamilton, London, 1956, pp. 11-38.

Rubin, Joan. Bilingualism in Paraguay. *Anthropological Linguistics*, IV, i (1962), 52-58.

_____. "Language and Education in Paraguay," in J. A. Fishman, C. A. Ferguson, and J. Das Gupta, (eds.), *Language Problems of the Developing Nations*. Wiley, New York, 1968.

_____. *National Bilingualism in Paraguay*. Mouton, The Hague, 1968.

Rustow, Danknart A. *A World of Nations: Problems of Political Modernization*. Brookings, Washington, D.C., 1967.

Schegloff, Emanuel A. "Sequencing in Conversational Openings," in H. Garfinkel and H. Sacks (eds.), *Contributions in Ethnomethodology*. Indiana University Press, Bloomington, in press.

_____."The Turn to Talk," in John J. Gumperz and Dell Hymes (eds.), *The Ethnography of Communication: Directions in Sociolinguistics*. Holt, New York, 1971.71.

Schnore, Leo. "The Rural-Urban Variable: An Urbanite's Perspective," *Rural Sociology*, XXI (1966), 137.

Sjoberg, Andree F. "Socio-cultural and Linguistic Factors in the Development of Writing Systems for Preliterate Peoples," in William Bright (ed.), *Sociolinguistics*. Mouton, The Hague, 1966, pp. 260-276.

Smalley, William A. Orthography Studies: Articles on New Writing Systems. United Bible Societies and North Holland Pub. Co. (1964).

Sorensen, Arthur P., Jr. Multilingualism in the Northwest Amazon. *American Anthropologist*, LXIX (1967), 670-684.

Stern, Theodore. "Three Pwo Karen Scripts: A Study of Alphabet Formation," *Anthropological Linguistics*, X, i (1968), 1-39.

Stewart, William A. *Non-standard Speech and the Teaching of English*. Center for Applied Linguistics, Washington, 1964.

_____. "Sociolinguistic Factors Affecting English Teaching," in Roger

W. Shuy *Social Dialects and Language Learning.* NCTE, Champaign, 1965, pp. 10-18.

_____. "A Sociolinguistic Typology for Describing National Multilingualism," in J. A. Fishman (ed.), *Readings in the Sociology of Language.* Mouton, The Hague, 1968, pp. 531-545.

Tabouret-Keller, Andree. "Sociological Factors of Language Maintenance and Language Shift: A Methodological Approach Based on European and African Examples," in J. A. Fishman, C. A. Ferguson, and J. Das Gupta (eds.), *Language Problems of the Developing Nations.* Wiley, New York, 1968.

Tanner, Nancy. "Speech and Society among the Indonesian Elite: A Case Study of a Multilingual Community," *Anthropological Linguistics,* IX, iii (1967), 15-40.

Tietze, Andreas. "Problems of Turkish Lexicography," *IJAL,* XXVIII (1962), 263-272.

Trager, George L. "The Systemazation of the Whorf Hypothesis," *Anthropological Linguistics,* I, i (1959), 31-35.

Twadell, W. I. "Standard German," *Anthropological Linguistics,* I, iii (1959), 1-7.

Valdman, Albert. "Language Standardization in a Diglossia Situation: Haiti," in J. A. Fishman, C. A. Ferguson, and J. Das Gupta (eds.), *Language Problems of the Developing Nations.* Wiley, New York, 1968.

Weinreich, Max. "Yidishkayt and Yiddish: On the Impact of Religion on Language in Ashkenazic Jewry," in *Mordecai M. Kaplan Jubilee Volume.* Jewish Theological Seminary of America, New York, 1953. (Also in J. A. Fishman [ed.], *Readings,* pp. 382-413.)

_____. "The Reality of Jewishness versus the Ghetto Myth: The Sociolinguistic Roots of Yiddish," in *To Honor Roman Jakobson.* Mouton, The Hague , 1967, pp. 2199-2211.

Weinreich, Uriel. Research Problems in Bilingualism, with Special Reference to Switzerland. Unpublished Ph.D. dissertation. Columbia Univ., 1951.

_____. *Languages in Contact.* Linguistic Circle of New York, New York, 1953.

_____. "Multilingual Dialectology and the New Yiddish Atlas," *Anthropological Linguistics,* IV, i (1962), 6-22.

Whiteley, W. H. "Ideal and Reality in National Language Policy: A Case Study from Tanzania," in J. A. Fishman, C. A. Ferguson and J. Das Gupta (eds.), *Language Problems of the Developing Nations.* Wiley, New York, 1968.

Whorf, Benjamin L. "Science and Linguistics," *Technology Review,*
    XLIV (1940), 229-231, 247-248.
_____. "The Relation of Habitual Thought to Behavior and to Lan-
    guage," in L. Speier (ed.), *Language, Culture and Personality.* Sapir
    Memorial Publication Fund, Menasha Wisc., 1941, pp. 75-93.
Wittermans, Elizabeth P. "Indonesian Terms of Address in a Situation
    of Rapid Social Change," *Social Forces,* XLVI (1967), 46, 48-52.
Wurm, S. A., and D. C. Laycock "The Question of Language and
    Dialect in New Guinea," *Oceania,* XXXII (1961/62), 128-143.

SOCIOLINGUISTICS

"The idea of systematic study of language as a social phenomenon is not new . . . But in spite of the recognition of language as a social phenomenon and the connection between linguistics and anthropology, the methods and insights of the social sciences and those of linguistics have generally gone their separate ways . . . In this introduction, however, Fishman has tried not only to represent all the major streams of research but also to integrate them as far as this can be done . . . he has succeeded in giving an unusually well balanced conspectus of the whole field . . . The social scientist will acquire a smattering of linguistics and perhaps a little respect for it, and the linguist will be lured on to the sociolinguistic theory and research methods which are more fundamental to his own discipline than he realizes."

CHARLES A. FERGUSON
from the FOREWORD

"Sociolinguistics is the study of the characteristics of language varieties, the characteristics of their functions, and the characteristics of their speakers as these three constantly interact, change, and change one another within a speech community."

JOSHUA A. FISHMAN
from the book

NEWBURY HOUSE PUBLISHERS
ROWLEY, MASSACHUSETTS 01969